THE SOVIET WAY OF CRIME

THE SOVIET WAY OF CRIME

Beating the System in the Soviet Union
and the U.S.A.

LYDIA S. ROSNER

Bergin & Garvey Publishers, Inc.
Massachusetts

First published in 1986 by
Bergin & Garvey Publishers, Inc.
670 Amherst Road
South Hadley, Massachusetts 01075.

6789   987654321

Library of Congress Cataloging-in-Publication Data

Rosner, Lydia S.
    The Soviet way of crime.

    Bibliography: p.
    Includes index.
    1. Crime and crimincals—Soviet Union—Case studies. 2. Jewish criminals—New York (State)—Brroklyn—Case studies. 3. Soviet Union—Emigration and immigraation—Case studies. 4. New York (State)—Emigration and immigration—Case studies. I. Title.
HV7012.R67 1986   364.2'5   86-6095
ISBN 0-89789-091

Manufactured in the United States of America.

To my parents, who left Russia during the second decade of the twentieth century, their romance with Russian literature and culture, and their insistence that their American children speak Russian and become educated Americans;

to my husband, my best friend, who encouraged me to move along avenues totally of my own choice and who supported my efforts, moods, and interests;

to my children, who thought it "great" that their mother did her own thing and listened to her problems and helped her in solving them;

to M.D., a woman of rare insight into her own Soviet and immigrant experiences; and

to my friends who said "do it" and then continued to provide needed encouragement, I dedicate this book.

Contents

Preface

This book is a study of Russian immigrants who have left the Soviet Union and come to the United States since 1973. Although this population has settled in many metropolitan areas, the primary focus of this study is the population that has settled in the Brighton Beach area of Brooklyn, New York. Of interest is the fact that these new immigrants come from a society that is more industrialized than the societies from which previous immigrations have traditionally come. This study examines these new immigrants and their criminal patterns in order to assess whether they are different from the preceding waves of immigration, whose origins were primarily peasant.

It will be argued that American theories of criminality are based on problems inherent in the industrialization, urbanization, acculturation, and assimilation of the peasant. In the process of urbanization, "ghettoization," and "detribalization," and in encountering a totally new environment, the peasant immigrants and their children—facing a myriad of new social and psychological problems—turned to anomic behavior and crime.

This book will provide us with a look at a new, Eurasian, urban population, already at least partly transformed by industrial society before immigration. This population will be considered as a possible example of a new type of immigrant who, coming from an already industrialized society, is urban, and has middle-class underpinnings and aspirations, but who is still engaged in crime. The social, political, and economic factors in the social structure of the homeland that may predispose the immigrants to crime there, and how they respond to similarities and differences in their homeland and new land with respect to criminal behavior, will be examined.

This book is divided into seven chapters. Chapter 1 examines criminal patterns in the Soviet Union by referring to the sparse literature on this subject as well as interviews with Soviet citizens. New immigrants from the Soviet Union are also interviewed with respect to criminal behavior in their homeland. It is argued that a criminogenic ethic already exists within the Soviet Union; and that at each level of Soviet society, daily activities are conducted amidst secrecy, illegality, and theft. This chapter details the pervasiveness, necessity, and contradictions of this criminogenic ethic and attempts to explain how this ethic is necessary for the survival of the Soviet individual. Because I am fluent in Russian and am able to employ the colloquial language, interviews with recent Russian immigrants provide back-up to the small amount of relevant literature available and indicate that there is a failure to control crime within the USSR. This failure results in a loss of ideological unity and in societal inefficiency. Examples will be provided in this chapter through the use of observational, experiential, and source materials.

Chapter 2 looks at the meaning of crime to the Soviet citizen. It examines the moral decisions involved in a monolithic, bureaucratic, urban society and looks at how an immigrant from such a society adapts his value system after immigration to another bureaucratic society. Since this immigrant is different from those of early immigrations in his experience of bureaucratic practice, it is necessary to look at those skills which are transferable to a new homeland. This chapter, additionally, draws comparisons between American and Russian understandings of these bureaucratic situations as they relate to crime.

Chapter 3 looks at the immigrant and crime, slums and cultural learnings within them, American criminal values, and the introduction of the concept which suggests that the criminal patterns of classic theories of crime and deviancy emerged in American cities, in particular the slums. The immigrants' old-world peasant patterns failed to enable them to cope with a new social reality, or they attempted to adopt new American aspirations while lacking, due to their peasant background, the means of achieving their newly established goals.

Chapter 4 encompasses an ethnographic study of the new Russian population after immigration. The adaptation of values, criminal and other, is examined through interviews with 35 Russian immigrants and others, particuarly law-enforcement personnel who have frequent contact with this population. Chapter 4 includes a chart summarizing the criminal understandings of this new population.

Chapter 5 suggests that the criminal behavior of this population differs from those of other previous peasant immigrations in that the skills and understandings encompassed by criminal activity within a bureaucratic society arrived together with the new Soviet immigrant. The earlier peasants came primarily from agrarian, prebureaucratic societies.

Chapter 6 defines the immigrants as either Survivors or Connivers. Each group is defined and their specific behavior is identified both in relation to their past experiences and to their present behaviors.

Chapter 7 draws conclusions from the previous material. It reexamines sociological theories as they have previously been applied to new immigrants, and contrasts these with theoretical perspectives that can be applied to the new immigrant from a technological, bureaucratic, and urban osciety.

I am aware that this study of the Soviet way of crime has both theoretical and methodological aspects that need to be addressed. The theoretical aspects are as follows:

1. Problems of bureacratization and urbanization have occurred in other parts of the world. Crime, as a result of these social changes, has also occurred in populations other than the one group under study here. The extent to which these findings are applicable to other immigrants to the United States, and within it to urban America, must be ascertained by other detailed studies of new post-industrial immigrations.

2. Soviet Russia is more extremely bureaucratized than most other nations that have sent immigrations to these shores, though in many ways it is less urbanized and industralized than most first-world nations. The thesis that immigrant crime reflects the degree of bureaucratization, urbanization, and industrialization of the Soviet Union homeland necessarily reflects the relative "backwardness" of the Soviet Union in all but its centralized, monolithic bureaucratization.

3. Soviet bureaucratization and Russian culture may have unique characteristics, which make comparison with other nations (that are the source of immigrants to the United States) problematic. The impact of these differences also awaits detailed research and assessment, and cannot be done in one study.

4. Despite these differences, some of the problems described here may occur among other recent immigrant groups. If this is true, it may be necessary to study the impact of bureaucratization and urbanization on other immigrant groups both in the homeland and in their response to the host country.

There are several methodological limitations:

1. There is a geographical limitation to those who could be interviewed. The Russian residents of Brighton Beach do not represent all Russian immigrants. Excluded especially are artists, intellectuals and higher professionals, who have not settled in the area. Nor is it a sample

of Soviet society in general. Its residents are primarily Jewish lower-mid-
dle and middle strata in Russia, with a few agricultural workers and
totally unskilled industrial operatives. In fact, it is quite possible that
Brighton is unique because of the concentration of people from one part
of urban Russia, Odessa, and not from many other cities. The new
immigrants may not be "typical" of all Russians; however, an examination
of crime in the Soviet Union has focused on factors within the social
structure that are common to all of Soviet Russia.

2. Certain people who were interviewed limited their responses to
direct questions because of their experience within their homeland with
agency officials who asked questions. Since there is no such thing as
independent research within a system where all research is done by governmental employees, immigrants from Soviet society often respond
with habitual caution to any sort of inquiries by outsiders. Thus, only
those who had personal relationships with me could be counted on for
openness. Even those who became part of a snowball sample (a technique
based on network familiarity) were often cautious in their responses.

3. Since the new Russian immigration has occurred only after the
1965 immigration and its bulk is less than ten years old, the full effect
of immigration on crime, especially in the second and third generations,
cannot be known as yet. Moreover, police and other law-enforcement
officials are only beginning to assess the amount and character of Russian
immigrant crime. Their assessment, as well as my own, is limited by
the reluctance of an immigrant to report crime to official agencies based
on the homeland habit of distrusting authorities.

This study paves the way for examination of other recent immigrations
and for an examination of the problems which occur in our own society
as a result of changes in bureaucratization and urbanization. The Soviet
society can be viewed as the extreme example of a society moving towards
total bureaucracy.

Introduction

Lydia Rosner presents a fascinating picture of crime in the Soviet Union and of how Soviet emigrés continue their criminal behavior in the emigré community in Brighton Beach, New York.

Crime is an essential ingredient of the way of life of virtually all Soviet citizens, Rosner reports. Top party leaders, NKVD leaders, state officials, regional party leaders, plant managers, and other officials loot state-operated industries for their personal and institutional gain. The ability to gain personal wealth, privilege, dachas, and diamonds rests on control of goods and services that can be illegally diverted from the state in exchange for other illegally diverted goods and services in vast and complex patterns of bribery and corruption and in subsequent mutual blackmail. The blackmail keeps the system in place: exposure of crime in one area of the system necessarily leads to exposure of the entire system. Thus it is understandable that Yuri Andropov and Mikhail Gorbachev have been concerned with official crime, bribery, "goofing off," and with the hoarding of labor and government supplies to meet phony standards.

Rosner reports that the level of official crime in the Soviet Union is so great that entirely illegal private industries have been created outside the Communist system. These industries supply unofficial services to the official servants of the state.

But the pattern of crime is not confined to the elite. At every level, those who can steal or divert official supplies do so. The salesgirl at GUM, the largest Soviet department store, may steal gloves to exchange them on the black market for fur hats, chocolates, oranges, or fountain pens. Ill people use stolen state property to bribe doctors to treat them quickly. Parents bribe teachers to "look after" their children. Taxi drivers bribe supervisors to assign them cabs that run. Officials bribe butchers to provide them with unauthorized choice meat. Complex patterns of bribery exist for the exchange of apartments and the purchase of used cars.

The amount of time spent dealing and trading goods and services stolen from the Communist state in the black and grey market may make the Soviet Union one of the great exponents of classical capitalism. The entrepreneurial activity at the interstices of state-owned industries may make those interstices larger than the industries themselves.

Rosner reports that, in order to survive in the Soviet Union at more than the minimum intake of calories, one must become a "necessary criminal." One must develop a "specialty" or trade that provides one with goods or services that cannot be obtained in legal markets. Rosner does not explain, however, the failure of those regular markets, except by noting that the fact of large-scale theft from the state machinery makes that machinery inadequate in providing the goods and services that would make the theft unnecessary. An alternative explanation might be that the vast state investment in military production and security services (14 percent of the Soviet GNP, compared with 11 percent of the American) deprives the population of civilian goods and services. Also, the Soviet policy of controlling legal prices leaves billions of rubles that can only be spent on the black market.

For the Soviet citizen, the consequence is that honesty results in deprivation. Some individuals, dissident intellectuals and religious believers, do remain honest, but at their own and their families' expense. Apart from these "innocents," vast numbers of Soviet citizens engage in crime. Their crimes include falsification of documents, forgery, and counterfeiting—the paper crimes that reflect a bureaucratic society. Rosner notes, however, that Soviet bureaucracy is not exactly the kind of bureaucracy that Max Weber described.

The paper crimes involve not only a class of necessary criminals, but also a group of more professional criminals, whom Rosner calls connivers. The connivers are experts in forgery, counterfeiting and the manufacture of documents. Necessary criminals, or survivors, and connivers are Rosner's major categories in her analysis of Soviet and Soviet emigré crime.

Rosner also argues that the Soviet system imposes other peculiarities on the crime conducted by its citizens. Since the major criminals are party members, state officials and law enforcement officials, the boundaries between enforceable legal norms and ordinary "necessary" crime are indistinguishable. When someone is charged with violating the law, the arrest is often the result of other circumstances such as political, ethnic or religious differences. In the absence of external standards of what constitutes illegal behavior and with few internal standards to guide him, the necessary criminal is forced to develop a code of behavior and the ability to interpret nuances and minimal cues to understand who is observing him and what pattern of illegality is being followed. This heightened awareness is a necessity, even if one is honest, in coping with a society in which the majority are criminal and in which prosecution for crime is arbitrary and unpredictable.

Given all of the above, the Soviet emigré comes to Brighton Beach with a predisposition to beat the system through crime. He purchases unnecessary papers such as a forged driver's license, and thus provides a market for connivers already skilled in the production of illegal documents and other forms of counterfeiting. The emigré also feels entitled to apply for all state benefits, whether he is legally entitled to them or not. Though well off, he may apply for welfare, housing assistance, food stamps, and other forms of aid. He learns to conceal his assets and provides the papers that would make him eligible.

In short, Rosner reports that a large proportion of Soviet emigrés bring to Brighton Beach social and psychological patterns of behavior and expectations imposed upon them in a crime-ridden society. They act out their homeland psychology in behavior that is gratuitous in Brighton Beach. In addition, American law enforcement agencies have found that the Soviet Union has deliberately exported with its Jewish dissidents a large number of professional criminals, spies and NKVD operatives. It is not clear from these reports whether the professional criminals among them are totally organized or are organized in "families" that have a coordinating committee called the Soviet Mafia of Brighton Beach.

It is clear that, at all levels, the Soviet criminal, whether necessary or conniver, is no unsophisticated peasant arriving in an urban society unprepared to cope with urban complexities and crowded ghettoes and carrying with him attitudes that make him and his children victims of the city. Like almost all immigrant groups that have arrived since the Immigration Act of 1965, the Soviet emigrés are urbanites prepared to deal with the problems of beating the system, especially its bureaucracy. They do, however, have blind spots: they do not understand due process, the rule of law, or the "coddling" of street criminals by the police. They also do not understand the multiple jurisdictions that govern law enforcement in the United States. As a result, Soviet emigré professional criminals use the airplane as a mode of conducting crime along with cooperation among geographically dispersed crime families, as they did in the Soviet Union, to beat the dispersed jurisdictional system in the United States. They are, however, surprised when inter-jurisdictional crime control agencies use computers to catch up with their dispersed crimes.

Rosner notes that all of these criminal activities exceed what we have come to expect from the basis of American theories of crime. She notes that Soviet crime is not the crime of peasants forced into alien and crowded ghettoes, but that of urbanites, sophisticated and knowledgeable in beating the system. It is the crime of citizens who know that the homeland official system is much more crooked than they ever were. American criminological theory, even before the rise of sociology and professional criminology, blamed the immigrant, the peasant, especially the most recent group to arrive here and his children, for violent crime, street crime, and professional crime. But one could argue that the major criminal in the United States since the Ofenokenochee land scandals and redemption of Revolutionary war-pay scrip has been the WASP establishment itself. Certainly, since the American Civil War, the railroads, banks, trusts, lumber interests and other environmental plunderers were the chief thieves of the resources of the United States. Entire legislatures have been bribed, sometimes repeatedly, by rival interests. Rosner reports that corporate criminals imported elements of the Sicilian Black Hand to break strikes, thus helping to create the Mafia in the U.S. But white-collar criminals have rarely been the object of sustained public attention.

Edwin Sutherland developed the concept of white-collar crime in 1930. He charged that virtually every major corporation is a professional criminal, as defined by the MacNaughton rule that defines one convicted of three felonies as a professional criminal. But Sutherland's concept of white-collar crime never really took. Instead, white-collar crime has been redefined as the crime committed by white-collar employees against the corporation. The corporation has, by definition, become virtually immune.

From time to time, Americans are shocked by great scandals. In Watergate, the Attorney General, like Vautrin in Balzac's *Comedie Humaine,* was not only chief of police but the chief of all organized crime. Vautrin was not Balzac's invention; he was a composite of two actual figures in early 19th century France. Attorney General John Mitchell was different in being the fall guy for a higher level but unprosecuted criminal.

We have also been shocked when manufacturers of electrical generators conspire to fix prices, when automobile companies bribe legislatures, and when the chief executive of an automobile company forms a private company to cheat the company of which he was president. We have also been shocked when the chief suppliers of the Pentagon are charged with systematic cheating on costs and prices. But we grow accustomed to the fact that individual white-collar criminals get a slap on the wrist, while the corporations as criminals are virtually immune from prosecution.

Perhaps, despite President Reagan's clamor for the spirit of individualism, the interpenetration of the military bureaucracy and defense supplier bureaucracies is so great that both kinds of white-collar criminals are immune from prosecution.

All of this is not unrelated to Rosner's report on Soviet crime. Rosner reports that the major source of Soviet crime is the regime and the Party; and I have emphasized her point that the original source of American white-collar crime is the corporations, aided by a corrupt government.

Do I overdraw the parallel between the two systems? Rosner stresses the reserve of Protestant morality that causes Americans to be shocked and outraged when highly placed Americans are caught cheating the system. This latent reserve of morality is, she argues, the balance wheel against total corruption. But the Communist ideals of egalitarism and of the "withering away of the state" are equally absolute, and in principle, ought to be equally strong counterbalances to official crime. But I suspect that the difference between the United States and the Soviet Union is not in the moral basis of their ideologies, but in the nature of their respective systems of law.

In the United States, the provisions in the Bill of Rights that protect a free press and offer some minimal resistance to government (despite McCarthyism and the Palmer raids) provide the basis for a tradition that includes the investigation of official and establishment crime. Investigative journalism "pays" and moral crusaders like Senators George Norris and Robert LaFollette, Sr. were elected because they opposed the establishment. One wonders if this is still true in the present, at least to the same extent.

In the Soviet Union, by contrast, a repressive official establishment has stifled all criticism of the Party and the state since the Revolution. The existence of official and petty corruption is thereby protected from exposure insofar as corruption is the reason for prosecution. The foxes guard the chicken coop.

Nevertheless, Rosner has raised a whole host of issues regarding white-collar and immigrant crime. Since the 1965 Immigration Act, virtually all immigrants from all shores have been urbanites well-equipped to subvert the law-enforcement bureaucracies, whether these agencies be criminal or honest. Many of the new immigrants have participated in organized criminal activities in their homelands. We have Colombian, Dominican, Cuban and Peruvian cocaine connections that supplement the American-Italian, American-Sicilian and American-Corsican connections of traditional stripe. The Southern Korean emigré, so far, has not to any large degree imported the currency manipulations perpetrated to get here. Only the South Korean government, the KCIA, and the South Korean Consul General's Office have engaged in crime, which is usually directed at Koreans living in the United States. It is too soon to tell whether Koreans will follow traditional immigrant patterns and produce their share of criminals along with the scientific, mathematical and musical geniuses they are already producing.

South Vietnamese refugees are in the same position: it is too soon to tell whether they, necessary criminals in their homelands, will develop that kind of marginality that produces geniuses, crooks, or both.

As for the Soviet emigrés in Brighton Beach, it may be too soon to tell whether the necessary crime they now engage in is a means towards gaining the wherewithal to become respectable citizens and white-collar criminals, or whether it is to become the base for a new, permanent criminal underclass in American society.

Joseph Bensman

THE SOVIET WAY OF CRIME

CHAPTER 1

Crime in the Soviet Union

Had the Cosmos Hotel been built in Miami during its heyday, it probably would have been aglitter and alight, full of tourists enjoying their visits and the sunny vacation atmosphere of people everywhere on holiday. Instead, it was built at 150 Prospekt Mira in Moscow in anticipation of an invasion of the press to cover the Moscow Olympics. Its crescent-shaped glassed front can be entered on two levels--either under the semicircular ramp leading to the main lobby on the second level, or under the ramp into a lower, less impressive room. Its public rooms and corridors have receptacles for a myriad of lights--an attempt at the creation of an American atmosphere. The bathrooms show hope of resemblance to moderately priced American motels but fail in even that simple aspiration. At best, the Cosmos Hotel would not create much excitement in 1980 Dallas, Detroit, or New York, but it did in Moscow during its construction amidst the glow and confusion of planning for Olympic games. Of course, the American press was never housed in these neo-American Russian quarters. The U.S. decision not to participate in the 1980 Olympic Games left the Cosmos Hotel like a spurned bride, waiting for her groom.

The Cosmos Hotel can provide us with a microcosmic view of life in the Soviet Union. Through a contractual arrangement, a

French firm was hired to design and supervise construction of this edifice. Cement, nails, lumber, and various other construction materials were to be provided by the Soviets so that the building could meet its deadline--the invasion of American journalists. A French woman engineer, who spoke fluent Russian, was to supervise. The construction workers and their supervisors were of two nationalities, Russian and French. Although delays are part of every construction job and redesigns and replanning plague every phase of building, raising both costs and blood pressures, the problem of delay on the Cosmos job was a bit different. Supplies often did not arrive. If they arrived for one phase of the work, they were so short on another that construction would halt. The French, not used to this particular method of construction, finally arranged to ship in supplies in order to finish the job as promised and as close to deadline as possible.

Even this method proved fallible. At piers and loading points, supplies disappeared. This kind of pilfering occurs wherever there is construction, but this pilfering was of such large proportion as to greatly slow down the construction of the building. Most of the pilfering was done to order, in such large proportion as to make it systematic theft. Party officials, who assigned particular workers to be employed on this site, would direct them to deliver particular materials to construction jobs in which the officials had personal interests. Even these workers helped themselves to a bit of the materials on the principle that if it's okay for him, why not for me?[1]

Konstantine Simis, writing in his book *USSR: The Corrupt Society*, says, "Underground enterprise is a positive tumor of corruption. Like a drop of water, it reflects the whole world of Soviet improbity. Just as the human body cannot live without air, underground private enterprise could not survive except for the fact that the Soviet state and society alike are rotten with corruption from the top to bottom."[2]

The results of all this "private" enterprise within the building of the Cosmos Hotel were evident to me when, accompanied by my mother, who is originally from Russia, I stayed at the Cosmos. It was in November 1980, just three months after the American-avoided Olympics. We had returned from a week in Odessa and Kishenev. We had toured alone in Russia and without a group, although met at every point of embarkation and arrival by an Intourist guide who would inform us of the hotel that had been reserved for us (there is no such thing as pre-reservations in the Soviet Union). Nevertheless, we were both fluent in Russian and, as often as we could, we avoided the erstwhile companionship of our guide and traveled alone. Our arrival at the Cosmos Hotel was timed to meet a group tour for the following week and, together with them, to leave the Soviet Union. After being assigned rooms, we were told that our tour group and leader would be arriving from the airport shortly and we were to meet in the dining room below.

We were ushered to our table by a surly captain and told that we might as well eat because the group was quite late already. The table, at the far end of the large dining room, was set with what appeared to be a full table service. Around us were other tour groups, mostly internal Russian travelers. We were fed the usual *zakuski* (appetizers, a major part of every Russian meal) and Chicken Kiev. Then we sat around and waited. Our waitress, a chubby, overly made-up blonde, bustled around us, learning our business while rearranging the setups for the forthcoming guests. After quite some time, the captain and our waitress had a major conference, joined by a black-suited messenger from the front desk. The waitress then informed us that the group had been delayed, would probably not arrive until well after midnight and that we should go to our rooms or out, as we wished. We chose to remain for another cup of coffee.

At that point I watched a peculiar ritual. The waitress opened the bottom door of her service cabinet and removed from it the eight neatly folded and piled napkins, which had been stored there awaiting the arrival of our companions. She then added to this unused pile our two soiled ones and returned all ten to the kitchen. She counted all ten glasses from our table and placed them on a tray for return to the kitchen along with all the remaining utensils and plates. Prior to this behavior, had the other guests arrived as scheduled, they would have had to ask for napkins. Those not requested would have been hers--remaining in the service cabinet; if asked, she would have had the perfect excuse that the guests had obviously stolen them. I have discussed this observation with those who have come from the Soviet Union recently and they have confirmed my reading of what had happened.

We entered the hallway with its ceilings meant for hundreds, if not thousands, of bulbs. Two were lit; the other receptacles were empty. The halls, miles of them throughout the hotel, were eerie and full of shadows. The bulbs had either never arrived or, having arrived, had been rerouted at some point between the pier and the sockets. We returned to our rooms.

The bathrooms turned out to be a caricature of those at Holiday Inns in America. Ours was blue-tiled--except here and there, at random locations throughout, where tiles of pink or yellow were interspersed. No pattern was intended. Instead, serendipitous innovation was evident. Our blue-tiled bathroom had developed a personality of its own, a random pattern of other-colored tiles replacing in all but one spot--where indeed there was no tile--the planned and designed blue dimension. Tiles provided for our blue bathroom had obviously found their way to some other privately built blue bathroom, somewhere else in town--perhaps to a dacha of a high official who had requested a set amount of blue tiles, perhaps to the bathroom of a worker, or to the worker's fruit seller, or meat-market manager, or school principal--the possibilities are endless.

It is difficult to assess either from my visit or from discussions with M.D., a recent immigrant who is familiar with the building of the Cosmos Hotel, whether the number of tiles missing from my bathroom were indicative of a major diversion of blue tiles into private enterprise building or whether they had been pilfered in a random fashion because of the personal whims of the personnel on the building site.

The faucets did not match, nor in fact did they offer a dependable supply of hot water. In addition, somewhere in the planning phase the waste pipe that was supposed to rise from bathroom to bathroom, connecting each individual toilet to a main pipe, somehow had managed to arrive in our bathroom in the wrong spot. Our toilet sat almost a foot away from its intended hook-up, and the hook-up itself sat alone, capped and useless in the middle of the blue-tiled floor with a jerry-rigged improvisation visible above the floor tiling.

Throughout this new structure there were rents and tears, compromise and change, and nothing or nearly nothing worked as planned. Even the dramatic driveway, the circular ramp leading up to the main lobby, was closed to traffic. The cement, we were told, could not hold up the weight of the buses and cars. It had been weakened through lack of basic materials in its mixture and was of insufficient strength to be serviceable.

Hedrick Smith explains how this situation was possible. He quotes a chemist describing how one can obtain government building supplies.

> The easiest way is to go out on the Ring Road, you know, the big circular highway around Moscow--pretend you need a ride, and wait for one of those big cement mixers. . . . You ride with him a while and then tell him, "Look, I need some ready-mixed cement. How much is it?" He nods, asks you how much you want and you agree on a price. For me, the driver delivered it right to my garage. In a few minutes, the deal was done. He had ten rubles in his pocket. I had my cement and there was still a lot left for his construction project. Nobody noticed, nobody cared. The concrete didn't belong to anyone anyway.[3]

It appears that this sort of crime and corruption and its resultant inefficiency are such a constancy in Soviet life because of the shortages that are rampant there. Harrison Salisbury, in his recent book, *A Journey for Our Times,* describes the Russians' prediction to buy whatever is available. On the streets of Russia, anyone carrying large boxes or crates, or bags with either soft or hard goods, causes an instant queue just by stopping on a corner and setting down his goods. Lines appear everywhere; almost magically everyone seems to sense that something is for sale. Salisbury describes how the shortages are a barometer for the Soviets:

> The response was always the same: Buy anything. . . . I could plot the rise and fall of the economy by shortages and surpluses in the stores--an abundance, say, of expensive clocks and a shortage of pots and pans meant more metal going into guns, less for the consumer. If sausage began to disappear, I knew the harvest was bad and Moscow was stocking up for a hard winter. If there was nothing for sale at the women's underwear counter, if every woman in Moscow was hunting frantically for bras to contain her robust bosom, I knew the cotton crop in Uzbekistan had failed again. I could follow the fluctuations in foreign trade. . . .When I found more sidewalk vodka than white-aproned country girls selling *morozhenoye* (ice cream), I knew that the dairy industry was doing badly and the government was pouring vodka into the trade system to increase its revenues (and to cater to chronic Russian alcoholism).[4]

Leonard Silk, writing in the October 9, 1983, issue of *The New York Times Magazine*, echoes Salisbury's observations. Looking at the Soviet economy from his vantage point of both economist and journalist, he describes his first-hand experience in trying to obtain a Russian-English dictionary in the capital's largest bookstore, and with no greater success in every city where he visited. He describes lines for cucumbers, cabbages, and other consumer goods. He then quotes a Soviet economist as explaining that the cause "lies in the outdated nature of the system of industrial organization and economic management, or simply in the inability of the system to insure complete and efficient utilization of the workers and of the intellectual potential of the society."[5] Silk barely touches on the magnitude of the problem of corruption, even though he sees a comparison between the Soviet situation and that in America's bureaucratic army:

> For ideological reasons, prices on goods in everyday demand are generally set below the level at which supply would equal demand; hence the hordes of people buying everything on sight. Excess demand makes it possible for Soviet industrial enterprises to be sunk in inertia and fouled up in red tape, and still survive. A Soviet business firm does not have to keep costs below selling prices and make a profit. What it does have to do is acquire labor, materials and transportation to fulfill the production quota it received from above. To prevent it from going broke in the process, it can be bailed out

in a variety of ways. The managers' success commonly depends not on how well they manage but on whom they know out there, and up there.

. . . Each enterprise seeks to solve its problems by taking labor, materials, equipment and capital away from other businesses and industrial sectors. To do this, it uses *tolkachi* --pushers, what we used to call dogrobbers in the United States Army. Since all businesses do it to each other, they collectively intensify the shortages, bottlenecks, waste and low productivity of the entire system.[6]

Yet this type of behavior is compounded by the fact that although money is paid in salary, banks are distrusted and possessions and goods for barter (often stolen or diverted) become a factor of everyday life. In a nation whose system presumes to provide for all its citizens and where the concept of private enterprise does not exist in either public or official speech, there is a large amount of private business. The worst curse that can be uttered in Odessa is, "May you have to live on your income." So pervasive is this underground *na levo* ("on the left" or black-market) economy that there is general agreement that oldsters, those who have been pensioned off the work rolls, have no way to survive unless they can find some additional means, either from family or illegitimately. Unless one is able to engage in this *na levo* economy, one is left to live on a governmental allotment, and one's existence is at a most minimal level. To supplement their income, Soviet workers must be in a position where they can physically handle some sort of commodities, be they foodstuffs, clothing, mechanical tools, paint, or supplies for industry. With these, workers can supplement their income through participation in the "free market." Among the illegal ways of supplementing the Soviet family budget, the most common is to steal from one's workplace. Over the 60 years of its existence, the Soviet economic system has failed to meet the needs of the population for food and decent clothing, both of which are constantly in short supply. It is natural then, that these are the most popular items to steal from wherever they are produced, processed, or stored.[7]

My informants ranged in age from young to old. Most had never been part of the Soviet elite, although several were able to travel extensively outside of the Soviet Union, therein certifying their privileged position. One might assume that those whose positions in the power structure are such that they have a vast amount of material goods, dachas, servants, and such, would not be part of this large-scale rearrangement of goods and services described as part of the *na levo* economy. Yet Konstantin Simis describes the lives of the privileged few as being involved in different but just as creative corruption as that done by the general public.

Simis describes the *Kremlyovka stolovaya* (Kremlin canteen), which can be used only by people with special passes who are recognized as the elite--higher army and security, party officials, state officials, distinguished actors, and academicians, their personal staffs, and their families. Payment in this Kremlyovka is made through vouchers that can be used either in the dining rooms or in the stores that are presumably filled with the highest qualities of foodstuffs and delicacies--many produced on state farms exclusively for this purpose. People who shop here look with disdain on 'town' food, as they call it, because of its inferior quality and expensive prices. Food at the Kremlyovka is discounted for the elite, whereas the general population gets not only scarce supply but also inferior goods at higher costs. The vouchers can be used in two ways. One is for the purchase of prepared meals in the Kremlin dining room, where, in addition to a first-class dinner prepared with superior food, the diner is handed a package to enjoy for lunch and supper. The second way in which the voucher can be used is by buying food in the Kremlin stores. Here the same vouchers will feed a family of four for a month. Simis reports that "such privileged families ate incomparably better on 80 rubles a month than an ordinary rank and file family could eat on 250 rubles, for whom even meat, chicken, and sausage are hard to come by in sufficient quantities, and expensive delicacies and fruits are out of the question."[8] Nevertheless, the ruling elite, although steeped in perquisites and privileges, are involved in the "universal corruption that reigns in the Soviet Union."[9]

At a lower level of corruption, removed from the lofty eagle's perch of Politburo privileges, is the District Mafia. It is interesting that, here in the United States, newly arrived immigrants have pointed to particular people and referred to them as Mafia. At first I thought of the term as a newly acquired Americanism, or perhaps a term used by the Soviet press to describe the kind of people who run this country. Only later in my research did I learn that an organized crime contingent existed in the USSR. This organized crime contingent bears no relationship to American organized crime, which is organized along family or structural lines. Organized Russian crime bears a resemblance only in its muscle, power, and corruption of the use of legal procedures. The Politburo population, with its rank and power, its ability to live on a plane beyond reach of the rest, confines itself to Moscow and the surrounding areas. Its strength comes from the Kremlin and its hangers-on are primarily involved in a whole network of special services, special stores, hospitals, and other areas leading toward delivery of goods and services. The Mafia power is District power. Konstantin Simis explains how the special distribution system operates:

In large cities too, such as regional centers, capitals of republics, and Moscow itself, the local ruling elite takes advantage of its position to obtain tributes. In these places, however, the tribute system takes on a somewhat different form and operates much less blatantly than its rural counterpart. But despite the fact that the regional or central administration may be in close proximity, the system is still unchanging and ubiquitous in large cities.

Information about this urban version of the tribute system never leaks out into the Soviet press, and I know of no case of a top employee of the party state apparat being prosecuted for having taken advantage of it. . . .The district elite in the large cities have free use of automobiles belonging to the various district institutions and enterprises, and of garage services to repair their own cars. Lacking in the large cities are the collective and state farms to provide the elite with produce, but this function is performed by the state stores and restaurants.[10]

These stores and restaurants were involved in a payoff system superimposed on what appeared to be the regular business of the day. Members of elite groups would appear for their provisions after first making a list of requirements and would have their orders filled while they waited in a back room. Their prices were less than those on the open market and yet the managers of the various stores and restaurants managed to make up what would appear to be losses through paper manipulation, that is, judicious juggling of books, cheating in reports, showing less delivery than there actually was, and so on.

Simis detailed the ties between organized crime and the Party machinery as follows:

Massive and ubiquitous corruption at the district level of the party state apparat has forged such close ties between it and the criminal world that there is every justification for saying that a system of organized crime has come into existence in the Soviet Union, a system that has permeated the political power centers of the districts as well as the administrative apparat, the legal system, and key economic positions.[11]

This system of district corruption has three layers. First, there are those who are all members of the elite, the party, and who manage stores, restaurants, collective farms, and various other respectable and necessary parts of any economy. They are involved in an illegal system together with the second component of this Mafia--lower-ranking members of the ruling party. The third part of this system is that these persons, in addition to their primary role as legitimate members of a ruling elite, have taken on the role of enforcers, pushing those below them to involve themselves with a corrupt system.

My informants suggest that there is a violent fringe to this kind of enforcement. If goods and services are promised and not delivered, if money was to trade hands and does not, it has been suggested to me that "thugs" are available to ensure that promises are kept. R.B., who is part of the new Russian immigration, discussed the concept of enforcement and of strong-arm tactics. "It is a good idea to only know your part of any deal. To know too much is dangerous." She acknowledged that there are enforcers among the "new" Russian immigration who held the same positions within the USSR.

Bribery cases are periodically tried in the Moscow courts and newspapers carry the stories. Simis explains taxi bribery as follows: the depot manager is the first one the taxi driver has to bribe in order to assure that he will get a good car. He also has to bribe the mechanic, who has to inspect the vehicle as to whether or not it needs service. If it needs service, he has to bribe him for promptness and then "buy" the parts from him. Two or three rubles then go to the controller to arrange for a favorable shift and then a couple to the car washer. Last, he has to bribe the gatekeeper, who must certify that cars are in proper condition and may then exit. The taxi driver's last bribe to the gatekeeper is part of an official payment, of which the gatekeeper can keep 100 rubles for himself and must then divide the rest among the depot manager, the chief engineer, the chief mechanic, the party committee secretary, and the chairman of the Trade Union Committee. Yet "another portion continues its ascent to the main Automobile Transport Administration of the Moscow Executive Committee and to the transport division of the Moscow Communist Party Committee."[12] Where the taxi drivers obtain this kind of money is in itself a further study in official and unofficial corruption. Their wealth is limited only by their lack of resourcefulness.

R.S., an American who speaks Russian, tells of waiting at the airport to depart for the return trip to the United States while the Soviet customs men tried to extort $200 in overweight from the 30 members of her tour group. They kept insisting that the luggage was too heavy, but she says, "There wasn't enough there [in the USSR] to buy to be $10 overweight." One of the Americans tried to suggest that perhaps it was the samovar he had bought, but surely it did not weigh that much. R.S. insisted that they would not pay. Two Texans, she relates, were more than willing to pay just "to get into the air," and the customs men were surly and brusque. They could not bring the luggage to be reweighed, they snarled, because it was already on the airplane. Only the fact that R.S. was both fluent in Russian and persistent saved the situation. They hauled the baggage back off the plane and into the shed. "I

would not take no for an answer. That's the only thing they understand, conduct which bullies." The baggage was overweight in the
amount of several rubles. The group paid and was finally allowed to
board.

R.S. was not permitted to board with the group. She was
subjected to a frightening hour, alone in a locked room. After
waiting there without knowing what was to happen to her, an
official finally arrived and confronted her. "I told him that I had to
return to the United States with my charter group and he said not
to worry, the flight would not take off without me." She related
how after being strip searched and chastised by unpleasant
officials, she was released. "I knew that they were punishing me
for proving them to be wrong about the baggage." She concludes
her story with the fact that she and her charter group of Americans
applauded when the plane was finally airborne.

Immigrants who have heard this story express no surprise at the
blatant quality of the extortion attempt. "There is push and shove
in every dealing with bureaucracy," says M.D., who, although un-
educated, has what C. Wright Mills would call "a sociological
imagination." She has a natural ability to examine systems and has
proven particularly perceptive in discussions of Russian bureaucracy:

> You see, no one takes responsibility. It is always the other
> guy who is responsible and therefore no good and no bad can be
> placed at your feet. Everyone knows that there is corruption.
> Everyone knows that anyone who has a chance will line his or
> her family's pocket. Everyone looks out for those important to
> them and does not care about the others. And everyone
> grumbles all the time and is sour because they think all the
> time and are careful all the time.

It is perhaps best to divide the life of a Soviet citizen into the
various components necessary for survival: food, shelter, clothing,
and health care, and then to examine how each aspect of that life is
affected by the totality of the corruption in the system. Of course,
corruption exists in the United States, and the bribe, the shoddy
workman, the pilferer, exist in many spheres. The primary
difference between America and the USSR is the extent, the
amount, and the way every aspect of one's daily private and public
life is affected. In the Soviet Union, no area of life is exempt from
the pervasive corruption.

PAPER MANIPULATION AND FOOD

Hedrick Smith recalls that he and his wife were having dinner with
a young biologist and Smith commented that the meat was tender

and better than that which was available in the state stores. The biologist explained to him that he had a friend who worked in one of the stores specially provided with superior quality food because it was in a neighborhood near where many VIPs live. A transaction in Russian stores has three stages: first you go to the counter and see what is available, then you purchase a chit for the amount you want to buy, and once again you return to the counter to exchange the receipt for a purchase. Smith's biologist had developed a system where he would pick up a receipt for 20 kopeks. Then he would wrap a 3-ruble note inside his receipt and give it to his friend who worked behind the counter. He would get the meat; his friend, the money; and the state store, the same 20 kopeks it would have in any case. By shorting others, the butchers could carry on a private business on the side. The butcher's position, which allows him to decide who gets meat and who does not, commands much authority and allows him access to other scarce commodities through a system of barter and exchange.[13]

I saw the inequality of state food distribution in a variety of neighborhoods in Moscow. I was taken to stores with no food on the shelves. It is hard for an American to imagine a store with counter and shelves empty but for canned olives from Afghanistan stacked pyramid fashion, a wire basket standing on the floor containing rotting lettuce, and an 1930s-style icebox holding only odds and ends of dairy products. Nothing else was in the store except a smiling, buxom salesperson visiting with friends and happy to pose for a picture.

Other neighborhoods, close to the center of Moscow, had bakeries and stores filled with products and people--although close examination showed that many of the displays were of the same items placed in different parts of the stores. My informants suggest that those areas peopled by tourists and those areas near where the VIPs live have the largest inventories. They all agree that the arrival by train of farmers with produce creates an immediate queue, no matter the neighborhood.

My informants also agree that if a manager of a particular store is skilled at manipulation, better at bartering, or has developed a solid network of friends in high places, then his store will be better stocked, with more frequent deliveries and a better quality product. D.R., who was a lawyer in the Soviet Union, describes the knowledge necessary to survive in the manipulative arena of the Soviet goods-and-services exchange: "The ordinary citizen knows that to be truthful and honest means to die of hunger. Therefore, there is created in the USSR a unique citizen. One who is socialist in public and capitalist in private. And the further from Moscow one goes, the less socialist and the more capitalist one is."

M. is a white-haired, dimpled woman in her sixties. Her life in the USSR included a stint in Siberia during World War II. Upon her return to Moscow, she found that without proper residence papers (hers were still officially registered for Siberia), there was not one person who would take her in, nor the two sons she had with her. She could visit here and there temporarily, but as she was without the necessary documents entitling her to live in Moscow, it was apparent that she was required to live someplace else. In order to live somewhere--anywhere--in the USSR, you must have documents so stating. These documents then entitle a citizen to food, clothing, shelter and employment. Since she had no documents at all, she was not entitled to live anywhere and could not remain where she was. Additionally, her friends were endangering their own positions by allowing her to stay with them for any extended period of time without her having the proper documentation. Without the precious residence documents, she had no legal way of obtaining food and no way of obtaining work in any city in the Soviet Union. M. and her two sons were actually nonpersons. What they did was what many people in that country had to do: they had to enter into the world of the paper manipulator where, for an agreed-upon price--money or services or goods--they obtain proper papers.

Through the use of wit and manipulation M. obtained not only her documents, but also a job as a cook in a children's nursery school. This provided her not only with food (3 meals a day in the school), but also with a sort of living accommodation. She explains that she was, in the end, like a skilled high-wire performer. No circus tightrope walker could equal her dexterity. She was suspended in space, constantly moving back and forth between two points. Her problem was that since she had large amounts of food delivered to her, enough to feed breakfast and lunch to a school full of children, she commanded a useful commodity. District officials would turn to her for handouts. She was expected to provide many around her with extras for their families, to grease the palms of the suppliers of food with tidbits of food for favorable supplies, and yet she had to feed a school full of children. Her tightrope act was constantly shaken by the fear that the children, whose soup was perhaps too watery or whose bread was not sufficiently buttered, might discuss this with their parents. If she did not pay off, there would be less food for barter. If she did, there was less food for the students.

A recent Russian immigrant first tasted a dark-colored liquid at my home and then inquired, "What is this?" "Pepsi," was the reply. "I thought there was Pepsi in the Soviet Union also." "Oh," she countered, "there is, but of course it doesn't taste like this. You see, when the syrup arrives at the factory it is probably cut in half. Half is used to make the soda and half is distributed through some network for private use in other places. And the worker who has to deal with the syrup also has to take some for his business. So I guess ours is cut to at least quarter strength."

S., a graduate engineer, recounts how on weekends during

harvest season he was required to go out into the fields to help pick potatoes. "Imagine that," he says, "here I had to deal with these production and supply problems at work and then I couldn't even have weekends. I had to go pick for the good of all. Imagine how hard I worked. I was in no mood for farming. I picked a few potatoes for me, and for my mother who is old, and some for friends. But for the state--not many."[14]

HOUSING

A.E. is the pretty, twenty-eight-year-old mother of a ten-year-old daughter. She explained that her entire family, two sisters and their husbands and mother and father, were able to leave the USSR within one year. Her sister and husband emigrated first, but since the family is particularly close, the rest followed within eight months. Knowing that there are those who are denied request after request and wait for years before being given permission to leave, I inquired as to how difficult her wait was. "Oh, it was just a matter of maybe three weeks. We had a lovely apartment, two and a half rooms with large windows overlooking the park in Riga, and it was very desirable housing. Maybe the official wanted the apartment and that's why we were allowed to leave so easily." She continued to explain that in the same two-and-a-half room apartment had lived the whole family--the mother and father, the two sisters and their husbands and she with her husband and child, until her divorce. "Living in marriage is hard in such quarters," she explained. Hers is not the only story concerning apartment availability as lubrication for easy exit.

M.S., previously a lecturer at the Hermitage, recalls that "my parents had to die before I could have an apartment and that apartment was my inheritance because it permitted me to leave. We waited only four months. I think someone did very well on our apartment."

As M.S. states, it was less a factor of governmental policy that permitted her to gain the proper documents for exit than the need of some bureaucrat to possess an apartment. Robert Kaiser came back from the USSR with this realization as well. He explains that he saw self-interest as the basis for much governmental action: "Patriotism and idealism can be invoked by anyone, but I left Russia with the feeling that simple self-interest was usually the best explanation for the way Soviet officials behave."[15]

It should be understood that the apartments were not necessarily for the personal use of those officials who were responsible for issuing exit permits. Rather the system works in a chainlike fashion, with barters and exchanges of apartments (all with state goods and services) being the currency of the marketplace.

Since the housing shortage is so acute, at least for those who are not part of the ruling elite, the government has attempted to provide new housing. In a ring on the outskirts of both Leningrad and Moscow, I saw high-rise structures shaped like milk cartons, reminiscent of America's public housing developments of the 1960s. In the USSR they are located far from center city, new communities in the making, prefab nine-story, eleven-story, and fourteen-story monotones against the sky. M.D. explains that because her house was scheduled for razing, she was relocated into one of these new buildings, far from town.

She moved in before the building was finished--in fact, she reports that it was never quite finished. The water was not connected and neither were the elevators, no electricity and no gas were provided, and the faucets throughout the building were not in place. For five rubles she could get the superintendent to install them. "They couldn't leave faucets in empty apartments--they would all be gone before any tenants arrived." As to the gas and electricity, the hot water and the elevators, they were not operable until every apartment was occupied. The government was not interested in providing services to a less than full building. M.D. explained that the nine-story house built in the place of the one where she had lived, which had been razed, was soon tenanted with those with connections to higher rankers on the bureaucratic ladders.

When M.D. first arrived in the United States I took her to my house, located in the kind of suburban subdivision that creates instant bedroom communities. She walked through the dining room, the living room, and then the kitchen. She walked through the basement playroom. She studied the rooms with the kind of reverent quality which one might bring to church on Christmas eve. She paused and then asked, already knowing the answer, but finding belief hard to come by, "But, you have rooms that no one lives in. How do you manage that?"

Since there is a shortage in housing, as there is in virtually all consumer needs, the ability to control an empty apartment provides one with extralegal channels in which to navigate. Hedrick Smith comments that more than one-third of the people in the Soviet Union still live in communal apartments.[16] Thus it is understandable that officials with the ability to grant foreign exit permits would take into account the desirability of an apartment and exactly what it would bring on the *na levo* market.

SELF-EMPLOYED AND SUPPLEMENTARY WORK

M.R. was a house painter in the USSR. He is a descendant of a Russian Jew who owned real-estate during the time of the Czar. His grandparents and aunts and uncles were doctors and lawyers, he reports, but he "favored" downward mobility. "You can do better for yourself that way and you have your hands to work with. Also, there is less hassle with the government." M.R., who immigrated four years ago, describes how he worked as a house painter. "You get sent to a job with a team of five. You bribe the superintendent and then only two of you stay there to work. Two others go someplace else, where the superintendent can keep the whole amount of allotment given for a *remont* (house painting done by state-employed workers), except for what we agree on as a price for our work. One other goes someplace else, where perhaps a private party wants some work done. At the end of the day we split the amount of money we made."

In addition to the income derived from such transactions there is the added bonus of controlling a supply of paint, brushes, and other tools of the trade. That means at the very least, that the apartment where the painter lives will be covered with paint which has not been watered, but probably so will those apartments of friends and family, as well as those of the private clients whose apartments he paints on a contractual basis in order to supplement his income.

It is important to understand that the ability to lay hands on goods means the ability to improvise. It means that one is in a better position economically. Those who are the intellectuals, who have less concrete materials to deal with, have a harder time improvising. If they are fortunate enough to travel outside the country, then they can return with foreign goods that allow them an additional source of income. A champion fencer told how he would return from abroad with skis and ski equipment for sale to those who wanted a better quality than that available internally:

> Because I was outside of the country for championships, I was able to take orders for things which were not available inside or which no one wanted because of the quality of Russian-made equipment. So I was in a good position to make some money by importing sports equipment. Everyone who goes outside is in a better position than those who cannot leave.

After questioning, he continued to describe how being a Russian athlete has supplemental benefits: "Even just going into Europe was wonderful. We came back with skis for skiers, and fencing things for fencers. And we were better dressed than the other people because we could buy clothes."

When in the USSR, I met the world-class Russian championship tennis team while in a restaurant in Kishinev. They stood out from the crowd because they so resembled Americans. Dressed in jeans and cashmere turtleneck sweaters, moving with a casualness that was non-Russian in quality, they looked out of place as they sat at a table and laughed and smiled and finally introduced themselves to me, also obviously out of place in the crowd. They confessed that they were most unhappy with their plight of recent days. No longer were they able to travel to the United States. Defections and the Soviet response to Carter's withdrawal from the Olympics had limited their scope of play. Now they only went to Africa, they said. On the dance floor, where we could talk in Russian and not be overheard, the coach of the team expressed his sadness. No longer would he be able to be a somebody. As he aged, he could at best only hope that he would coach a junior team, but his traveling would be curtailed. Although he had been to Forest Hills and seen the States, he would be limited to life inside the Soviet Union. He despaired of his future. Not only would he slowly become a nobody, but also, as time went on, he would have a decreasing standard of living.

M.D. describes the activities of the *shabashniki* (the term comes from the word *shabashnichestvo,* meaning "self-employed"). These are the people who engage in the purest of free-enterprise activities either after they are through for the day at their main jobs or during the hours they are supposed to be engaged in state employment. They work hard, are creative, give service where service is needed, and perform "good" work in all respects. These people are hired, for example, to build structures on the collective farms. They arrange for materials destined for one site to be waylaid and sent to the one where they will work. They bribe those who control the sources of supply, then they send teams out to build or are part of a team that builds for the collective farms of a particular district. Simis describes the members of such a team, who had a permanent representative at a state lumber procurement station, as those "whose duties included obtaining lumber and having it shipped to the Stavropol region. [They] bribed the managers of the lumber yards to give [them] the timber, and [they] bribed the railway officials to give [them] the freight cars to transport it in."[17]   Such work is usually done outside of one's official job. M.D. tells of her neighbor who would take his vacation each year as part of such a team. Throughout the year he would stock his bedroom with nails, hammers, and necessary supplies from his job, which would enable him to complete his *shabashniki* work.

CLOTHING

To the American eye, the appearance of the people on the streets of Moscow and Odessa is monochromatic and somber. No bright red or orange is observable in their dress; and one sees little light blue or yellow. An Intourist guide explained to me how apparel was a problem in an economy based on future planning: "How can we compete in the designer market of clothes? We make our plans five years in advance. And then the factories have to get the material and the workers have to sew the clothes. It is hard to be Parisian with such constraints." She described how she was able to dress well. "I knit," she confessed. Because she was able to travel outside and because she traveled with tourists throughout the inside, she was able to obtain wool and to see current styles. She was caught in a dual problem in dealing with me. We were the same age. I was wearing a red goosedown vest which she coveted. Yet she had to spend our time together extolling the virtues of the Soviet system. At the top of the Potemkin Steps, at the Odessa harbor, breathtaking examples of an older regime, she clutched my arm and whispered in my ear. "What are they wearing in New York this season? Tell me."

Hedrick Smith recalls that one of his first impressions upon arriving in Moscow was

> that people were better dressed than (he) had anticipated. But when (he) began comparing what was actually on sale in stores, the two did not jibe. Obviously, there was more to shopping than met the eye. It was the under-the-counter bribery of sales clerks for those desirable and perennially scarce items that Russians call *defitsitny*, deficit goods.[18]

The practices of bribery and illegal commissions made on state-supplied goods are the very basis of the understandings that Russians have about shopping. I have already mentioned the preponderance of instant queues in Russia. Riding on a bus through a Russian city, one sees these lines either already formed or forming at several points of the trip. My Intourist guide left us at one stop to join such a line. "They have gloves from Hungary," she said. Those who are purchasing these items from such lineups are already at the end of the distribution system, for the seller has already supplied those of importance to him: friends, family, officials, favor grantors and such.

Lampooning this practice, *Krokodil*, the Soviet humor magazine, once did a takeoff on a floorwalker promoting some newly arrived items: "Dear customer, in the leather goods department of our store, a shipment of 500 imported women's purses has been received. Four hundred and fifty of them have been bought by employees of the store. Forty-nine are under the counter and have been ordered in advance for friends. One purse is in the display window. We invite you to visit the leather department to buy this purse."[19] The black market begins where price-scalping leaves off because, as *Krokodil* suggested, clerks themselves buy *defitsitny* items and then retail them illegally on their own time, or else customers hoard choice items and then resell them.

This black market, the one which deals with consumer goods, exists wherever there are people. There is no established site. Smith sees it as being everywhere and nowhere. It is, however, an understood, established way of doing business in the Soviet sphere. Informants have related that through custom, there are certain areas of the city where you might go if there was a particular product you were looking for. For example, the trade in women's cosmetics is restricted to a particular part of a Moscow street. There you will find exchanges of foreign cosmetics, either sent through parcels to relatives or pilfered from shipments destined for *Beryozka* stores (those which sell to foreigners and to others in the USSR who have U.S. dollars).

In addition to the corruption surrounding clothing and other manufactured items--toasters, lamps, and such--my informants relate that the informed consumer, indeed the totality of Moscow, knew to check the date of manufacture on each product. This date was of importance because each *kolkhoz* or plant is required to follow a plan--that is, an allocation that must be produced each month. Since it is in the interest of each plant director to underplan in order not to be caught short, there is much idleness on the job. Thus, goods manufactured during the first part of the month are worth buying. Those made after that tend to be incomplete. Once the allotment has been neared, workers and indeed plant managers help themselves to portions of material and parts, in order to be able to manufacture items on their own time for private trade. Everything is either diluted, divided, or fractionalized.

John F. Burns, writing in the June 22, 1983, issue of *The New York Times* describes this phenomenon as follows:

> Readers writing to *Sotsialisticheskaya Industriya* told last year of new cars that had to be towed off the lot because of missing batteries, improperly assembled gearboxes and other woes. One Zaporozhets owner told how he had his new car replaced on the warranty twice, but had not turned a wheel in four years because of defects. . . .
>
> Obtaining parts is a nightmare. The state runs a network of special over-the-counter stores, but the hoarding of parts for black market sale causes most of the supplies to be re-directed to the service centers run by manufacturers, where the customers are supposed to prove their need for the item.
>
> This creates new opportunities for unscrupulous service mechanics, who take payoffs of up to 10 times the state price to "find" a needed part in the stores and charge a fee to move customers' cars to the head of the line. . . .

One official estimated that 5 of every 10 cars are fixed "on the side" by free enterprise repairmen operating illicitly in backstreet garages, usually with stolen parts.[20]

A.E. is the daughter of the manager of a major motor-pool garage, where the government keeps and repairs cars that are distributed to factory heads, governmental middle-men, and others who may need a car for business. Because A.E.'s father controlled the dispensing of automobiles to those in need, he was in a most favorable position within the Soviet economy. He could create his own scale of worthiness and determine who had to wait for his car and who did not, whose car was quickly repaired and whose was not, and generally reign supreme over a motor empire somewhat of his own making. A.E. relates that her father "could call up someone and tell them that his daughter needs a coat," and a coat would be provided.

As a result of her father's position in the economy, A.E. relates, "We lived quite well. We had everything we needed and I was known throughout Riga by everyone. Here I was only seventeen and I could already drive. And we had a fancy sports car of foreign origin and to see me behind the wheel--of course I was known throughout the city. Imagine what a life we had." A.E. is the same informant who described how many people lived in her two-and-a-half room apartment: nine. She also suggests that one of the reasons that some people are able to get exit permits to leave the Soviet Union is because they were able to provide others with cash, goods, or services to the governmental bureaucracy involved in exit permits.

HEALTH CARE

S.R. describes the nurses and doctors as part of a large bureaucratic network who "have to work too hard for too little money," and says that they tend to lose interest in their cases. Because self-interest dominates the Soviet consumer system, the only way to ensure that a loved one is given medical care above the average--which is little care--is to bring gifts to those who have dealings with the patients. These gifts, *baksheesh*, which S.R. likens to tips in the United States, are also a reason to have on hand a stock of desirable items.

Not only is life in a hospital eased through a virtual black market of provider services, but also there is a black market in health care beyond that described to me as part of the state system. Those who are able avoid the state health-care system, and try to acquire personalized care through connections.

Just as there exists a world of private enterprise in goods distribution, so one exists in medical care. Medicines, like sweaters and gloves, are difficult to acquire. Contacts and illegal systems in the acquisition of both medicine and health-related products is a part of the system that claims to provide health care for all at state expense. Although my informants acknowledge that this care exists, they see it as noncaring and bureaucratic, with connections and bribes easing one's way through the system.

Robert Kaiser, in *Russia*, quotes a doctor he met in Rome who had just emigrated from the USSR:

> Because doctors are so poorly paid, they try to find alternative sources of income. This leads to a whole series of ugly and unpleasant complications in their relations with patients. The doctors want to get some extra money, but since this is illegal, the whole business takes on the character of some kind of black-marketeering.
>
> For instance, you have to have an operation, and you know that ordinarily it would be a three-week business-first tests, then the operation, then recuperation. But you want to get it over quickly, so you make a deal with the doctor, and both of you get what you want. But this is offensive to relations among doctors. You hear complaints--"So-and-so took too much, So-and-so didn't take enough," and so on.[21]

The health-care system thus takes on the coloring of the whole state-welfare system with its shortness of supply and the pervasiveness of the people's response, that is, bribery and theft, accusation and corruption.

THE PERVASIVENESS OF CORRUPTION

It is difficult to describe the corruption and criminal activity that occurs at the uppermost levels of Soviet society because those who are at that level are rarely open for interview and even more rarely choose to emigrate. However, there are some windows through which this world can be viewed. Konstantin Simis, who, until he emigrated, was teaching in institutions of higher education in the USSR and who was a trial lawyer engaged in many actions before the Soviet courts, describes just how pervasive the corruption is at all levels of the system. Through friends in high places he was able to gather material about the ruling elite and their activities. The major difference between those in high places and the rest of the population seems to be that the former are engaged in larger and more enterprising ventures in private capitalist economic life, employing the services of the rest of the population to provide them with the items needed for the continuation of their private enterprises. Provincial bosses extort goods for them. Their children obtain diplomas and entrance into the best institutions of learning without having to deal with competitive selection. (Examinations for selection are not written but oral, thus permitting a vast amount of leeway in decision.) The ruling elite is pyramidal in shape, with the ruling committees of each province being included in the next level of power, until at the very top of the pyramid are the

> top functionaries in the apparat of the Central Committee, the chairmen of the Council of Ministers and the Presidium of the Supreme Soviet of the USSR. . ., their deputies, members of the government of the USSR, secretaries of the central committees, and chairmen of the councils of ministers and presidiums of the Supreme Soviets of the fifteen Union republics.
>
> There are very significant differences among these . . . levels in terms of the limits of their power and official position; . . . However, the corruption of the Central Committee secretary, living in his government house and provided free of charge from special government stores with all the food he needs to keep his family, and the corruption of the secretary of a remote provincial Raikom, who has none of those legalized perquisites, have a common foundation. That common foundation is power, a power unbridled by the principle of subordination to the law or by a free press or by the voice of public opinion. It is the power of the party apparat that has turned the Soviet Union, in the sixty-three years of its existence, into a country eaten away to the core by corruption.[22]

This type of corruption at the top, so vast and so circumscribed because of limitations of public access, is understood by all those who live with the Soviet state. As J.P. said, in describing the elite, "they live in a country that is all their own, on top of the country we live in."

Intertwined with the corruption of governmental agents is the corruption and crime that are a feature of a vast network of industries and distributorships resembling those of the capitalist world in everything except their legality, their supply channels, and their efficiency. Although the KGB is fully aware of the corruption within the ruling elite, the members of this elite "remain inviolate." "The fact is that, since its inception, the Soviet regime has been tolerant of the ruling elite's improbity."[23] Since the members of this ruling elite often are put into the situation of playing hand in hand with underground businessmen, they are unable to resist pressures upon their professional activities as well. Simis describes massive corruption in Georgia, which included trading posts within the party and state apparatus. As a result of this, an underground millionaire was able to get himself appointed to the post of Minister of Light Industry. This millionaire was in the fabric business and manufactured and distributed materials. His desire to top his career with a public post was aided by the fact that he had had to bribe public figures in the daily operation of his business and thus was able to press for his desires.

It is surprising for us that there are underground millionaires within the Soviet State. Yet they exist, and every so often the Soviet press is rocked with scandal about such a millionaire's being caught. This creates a problem, because it is a certainty that that millionaire has been dealing with all levels of Soviet citizens in his business pursuits. Simis continues:

> During the trial of the Georgian Laziashvili, one of the biggest underground business figures in the country, the defendant's business agents provided the investigation and the court with a list of the people to whom bribes had been given. The list began with district police officials and went on to name heads of the DCMSP (including the chief of the Republic's DCMSP) and the Ministry for Internal Affairs (including the minister) and public prosecutors from the district level on up to the Public Prosecutor of the Republic. A prominent place on the list was occupied by employees-- from the lowest level on up to the ministers themselves--of the ministries on which Laziashvili's enterprises depended. The list of the state officials regularly bribed by Laziashvili was crowned by the names of the Chairman of the Council of Ministers and his deputies. But the largest bribes found their way to party rather than state leaders among whom were officials ranging from the first secretaries of the Raikoms to the first and second secretaries of the Central Committee.[24]

Since the illegal millionaire cannot spend his money conspicuously, by buying luxuries that cannot be explained to governmental questioners, other covert and illegal schemes are created. These illegal businessmen not only have to engage in creative bribery in the form of providing supply and labor for their illegal businesses, but they must also bribe officials to help them cover up their unexplainable amounts of money. For example, they might purchase a big-winning lottery ticket or governmental loan bond from the winner, by paying the owner two or three times the amount won. Or they may claim to have won at the races.

It is not surprising that with the various levels of think and super-think that must go on to conduct one's business within a society which is engaged in double dealings on all levels, one is constantly vigilant. When M.D. says "life is very difficult in the *Soyuz*" (*Soyuz* is the term used by Russians to describe the Soviet

Union), she is talking not only about material deprivations but about the amount of mental activity in which one must constantly engage to slip through the various levels of games and creations that are an essential part of Soviet economic life.

The ordinary Soviet citizen has become skilled in the interpretation of nuances and understandings related to crime and corruption. Every encounter and every endeavor are testing grounds for these understandings. These finely honed skills are used by the citizenry on almost a 24-hour basis. Only within the folds of one's own room can a citizen of the Soyuz relax. Even there, what with watchful landladies, communal kitchens, and curious neighbors, relaxation is hard to come by. The ability to search for nuances of meanings within the shadings of expression is part of the baggage of Soviet life. Skills vary within the populace, but Russians surpass the average American in such behavior. Nuances and understandings of the hidden meanings underlying each encounter, the safety of each proposal, and the what's-in-it-for-me are constantly balanced.

I became party to this kind of behavior throughout my stay in the USSR. Because I know the language, I could gauge the confusion encountered by my being there after President Carter's withdrawal of American participation in the Olympic games. For the average Russian, free travel, without governmental permission, is beyond imagination. This was the framework for interpretation of my being there with a large party of other Americans. To them the confusion stemmed from the following facts: Our President had said we could not go. Yet we were there. Either we were dissidents and therefore to be hailed as sympathetic to the Soviet endeavor, or we were there on some sort of quasi-official mission with American governmental approval. In that case we were obviously to be avoided, because we could evoke reprisals by the security forces among those who came into friendly contact with us.

These kinds of dilemmas are not part of the daily understandings of Americans. Rarely is there need for them. Rarely does the average citizen engage in such problematic thoughts upon meeting another person, either from his own world or from another.

SECRECY AND DECEIT

The Soviet Intourist guide is a master in the art of deceit. Throughout my stay in the Soviet Union I found that answers to questions did not necessarily mean what they seemed to. "Take a taxi," to the theater or zoo, seemed to imply that there were taxis in that town available for our hire. Indeed, not the case, yet guide after guide would describe the way to get someplace by taxi.

"I don't think there is a Jewish synagogue in Kishinev," said the fashionably dressed blond lady who had accompanied us throughout our day tour of that city. She had lived in the center of Kishinev all her life, she told us, but as American friends had pointedly suggested that we visit its synagogue, we pressed the issue. It was then and with great astonishment that our guide "discovered" that indeed there it was, right in her home city. What a surprise! She suggested that we check with the "service bureau" in the hotel lobby before we go wandering about, "so as not to cause you any trouble." When I asked her specifically what she meant, she smiled and suggested that it was for our own good that we check before wandering too far. The fact that I was fluent in Russian and that we had asked that "next" question (that is, the question a Russian would know better than to ask), presented both our guides and me with substantial problems.

Deceit exists at each restaurant table, when the waiter hands you a menu, allows you to look at it for a while, and then after you order goes into the kitchen and returns to tell you that they are out of that particular item. By the end of our trip, we had learned to hand back the menu and ask the waiter or waitress to tell us exactly what they did have. This game has been reported to me by all those who have visited the USSR within recent years.

FEAR

Those who have immigrated from the Soviet Union explain how fear of neighbors, fear of the building superintendent--whose job it is to report on tenants to the authorities--and fear of being accused of doing a wrong thing have all created a climate of evasion and distrust. M.S. describes how these fears wax and wane through political changes and how the populace, especially the intellectuals, look for barometers to predict the changing storm signals of governmental pressures. So pervasive are these feelings of being at risk that I, for one, after a week in Moscow, discovered myself in the following parody of a James Bond movie:

I returned to my hotel room after disobeying the guide and touring the city, together with two others from our tour group. (Disobeying our guide gave me and the other Americans on our trip a sense of exhilaration--almost as we had felt when cutting classes in junior high school.) As I placed my scarf on a high shelf of the closet, an American business card tumbled to the floor. I dropped it into the wastebasket and went out of the room on our daily tour. It bothered me all day that there, in my wastebasket, was a card from an American businessman whose name meant nothing to me and whose occupation, saddler, meant less. Would the *dezhurnaya* (the lady who is employed to sit on each floor of a Russian hotel as a monitor) find the card? What would she make of it? What was that man involved in? Was I being framed? When I returned to my room I found the card still in my wastebasket. I tore it into little pieces, soaked it, and flushed it down the toilet. A ridiculous action, most probably. Yet the climate of suspicion and distrust among those who deal with tourists and the foreign visitors is such, especially perhaps in times of international turmoil, that a form of paranoia overtook me. But are you paranoid if they are really after you? Other members of our group, non-Russian speakers, also began to whisper when saying something derogatory about the government, the hotel, the guides, or any other aspect of Soviet life. Thus I took on the mentality of being a criminal though I had committed no crime.

OFFICIAL LIES

This smog in Soviet life, so quickly inhaled by visitors, obscures all public truth. It is part of the very socialization process, that this type of approach to dealing with all but the closest family members and friends is a necessary part of existence. M.S. reports,
"During Stalin's time, we didn't tell jokes even at home. We were afraid our children might spill something about them in school or to their friends. Now it's easier there. We joke with family and friends but Stalin's time is coming back again."

Kishinev is the first city through which the Olympic torch passed after entering the Soviet Union. In anticipation of this event, and of the foreign newsreels and photographers that would document this event, the fronts of buildings were cleaned. New, modern structures were added to the city center; preparations included restoration, painting, and even window displays.

The window displays provide a good example of how the official Soviet mind undertakes deception. In each city we visited, in the prominent central commercial area were windows displaying bolts of fabric with yards of the same fabrics criss-crossed into an abstract, colorful window display. They hung on wires attached to the ceiling of the window opening, creating breeze-filled spinnakers. It was such a contrast both in color and richness to the other surrounding windows that it was hard not to notice the same touch again, in city after city: the same display, the same fabrics, the same hanging quality. Somewhere in officialdom this "Western" look of displaying goods was drawn up, written down and distributed to stores that were within view of the foreign visitor. Inside all the stores, the promise was betrayed. No fabrics, no goods and only a few surly salespeople. Its presence was an obvious deceit yet it was repeated over and over again for Western eyes.

Behind the broad avenues of Kishinev, dressed up for foreign Olympic viewing, were the very same rubble-strewn streets, the broken sidewalks, and general disorder that were there before the cleanup. The tour-bus driver, after the rest of the group had disembarked, hung his hat over his radio-speaker, walked to the middle of the bus, and whispered to us that everyone was involved in the cleaning and preparations. Great wealth had reached many hands because of the allotments of supplies for the shining of Kishinev for the foreign press. "We cleaned a little and we took a little and everyone was happy," he whispered.

These, then, are the public and private faces in Soviet daily life. At any given time, it is hard to be sure of the boundaries, because the political climate brings changes in the lines between safety and disaster. My informants all agree that it takes constant vigilance to ensure one's safety. In some fashion the Soviet citizen, in his public behavior, leads a surrealistic life, trying to determine the real from the synthetic truth. In addition to the cunning required to out-think the economic system, to provide one's food, shelter, and necessities, one must live constantly aware that whether out in public, around the superintendent of one's building, or near official agencies who create meetings and agendas for mandatory attendance, one must at all times engage in deceit or at the very least silent acquiescence.

Sergei Dovlatov, a recent arrival who worked as a newsman in the USSR before immigrating in 1979, describes how, as a journalist, he had to create and fabricate news stories upon direction of the authorities. He uses fiction to portray how his journalistic endeavors were most creative when he was trying to write the news. "Ten years of lies and dissembling. It's a hard road from the reported facts to the truth."[25]

PUBLIC AND PRIVATE WORLDS

Deception exists all around a Russian citizen and he or she has to learn to double-think each social and political item. M.D. tells me that during the American gasoline crisis, when many people rose early in order to wait in line at the pumps, there was a picture in a Russian paper of just such a line of cars. Next to it one could see a supermarket parking lot filled with cars. The caption was "Americans Abandon Cars Due to Lack of Gas." She relates that those who listened to broadcasts beamed from outside the USSR knew that this was not so, and yet would discuss it as if it were, should anyone else bring up the subject. M.S., a new immigrant, describes that reading the newspapers is a particular skill in the USSR. "We looked always between the lines for things which were not there and learned much in that fashion." In fact, several of the new Russian immigrants have expressed shock at the way our American newspapers tell of events that they feel should remain secret from the public. They are caught in the dilemma of the immigrant: the desire for change and the resistance to it.

On an Aeroflot flight from Moscow to Odessa I was seated next to a coal miner from the Urals. His pores were permanently blackened from coal dust, and his strong arms and hands were gnarled from the hard labor of the mines. The premoistened napkin I pulled out announced to him that I was not from his country. He leaned toward me and whispered, "Bastards! Last week an airplane fell from the sky and they haven't even announced it. Even the families don't know what happened yet."

DISTRUST OF GOVERNMENT

Underlying the public Soviet face, there appeared in private-- from those with whom we came into contact who shared confidences with us--a total distrust of governmental structure. This distrust was coupled with their understanding of an economic system that affected everyone and about which they were constantly hearing. In turn, citizens feel compelled to perpetuate the falsehoods. The Intourist guide who told us of the wonderful production capabilities of the *Kolkhoz* industrial plant she was showing us was the very same one who had conspiratorily asked, "What are they wearing in New York this season?" While she pretended to marvel at the production of her country, she knew that the stocks of Western stores were truly full.

Yet she could guide us with aplomb through a museum displaying the products of Moldavia. The museum, part of an industrial display complex built outside Kishenev, had four large buildings. The one we were in was virtually empty of products (a 4-H exhibit in any American town would include several times the amount of items displayed here in a governmental regional exhibit). The guide knew that this was minimal, I knew that this was minimal, and she knew that I knew that she knew. But with a sense of pride she persisted in pointing to the single display, there in the large glass case, informing me that this was being produced for sale in stores throughout Moldavia. I knew it was not so. She knew I knew it was not so. Yet the game was played out throughout each stop on our tour.

Implicit in the understanding of those who live within the urban centers I visited, and from where my informants come (and I speculate that this is so everywhere within the USSR), is the fact that trust is hard to gain. Double-think and creative ways of rethink are constantly being employed to sort out the truths of everyday life. Not only does a criminogenic ethic pervade everyday encounters--which is engaged in by all the citizens because it is now the principle underlying the economic distribution system--but government attempts to curtail this type of activity are themselves fraught with deceit and fabrication, adding layer upon layer to citizen's distrust. Thus, production figures as well as other channels of information are presented publicly to depict the state as successful despite shortages obvious to everyone.

It is then only a testimonial to the depth of the problem when Yuri Andropov himself attempted to reveal the amount of problems facing the economy. His statement that there is a "a national indulgence in smoking breaks, absenteeism and slipshod work"[26] is in itself deceitful. Ignored in the attempts to upgrade production is the fact that the underlying corruption in the economy prevents change. If each factory manager, deputy secretary, worker, and deliverer is engaged in a private self-interest-based, creative enterprise, then how much change has to be instituted in order for all of these cogs of the wheel to roll smoothly toward full economic production. Given, in addition, that the history of the Soviet Union is one of change and counterchange with an underlying history of corruption, it appears that the problems inherent in the economic system are greater than Andropov himself admitted.

Leonard Silk, in a *New York Times* article exploring the multitudes of problems in the Soviet economy, barely discusses corruption. In describing his meetings with Soviet economists in an attempt to find solutions to the problems in the economy, Silk reports that it was suggested to him that perhaps a solution would be to shift power to the factory level and away from the middle-level bureaucracy.

> This, in their view, will correct an unhealthy trend of recent years. According to the April memorandum of the Novosibirsk group, there has actually been a weakening of the powers of the State Planning Committee, at the economic apex, as well as of the industrial corporation and other economic enterprises at the bottom of the pyramid. "In stark contrast," the paper said, "the powers of the functionaries of the intermediate levels of management, the ministries and agencies have grown out of proportion, giving rise to departmentalism, to disproportions in the economy, to a growth of economic activity outside the formal economic structure." This last phrase apparently refers to that peculiar semiofficial underground economy in which bureaucrats foraging for scarce resources behave like bandits.[27]

Attempts to control crime have failed in large part because the very institution presumed to be upholding the legalities of the system is itself engaged in or has a large percentage of its members engaged in the same violations that it is publicly trying to eradicate. Yet, at the same time, the vulnerability of the enforcers in their private role is understood by all. The very structure of the system depends on a social myth that all must be involved in the good of the many. In admitting that there is indeed a criminal and corrupt aspect to a major portion of the Soviet endeavor, the government is involved in the admission of its own failed system. Although hints appear throughout the press, and an awareness of the economic woes of the country as partly a result of in-house theft and corruption are discussed on private plateaus, of necessity it is always the other guy who is doing the criminal activity and in many ways the describer is really the very same "other guy" whom he is describing.

Konstantin Simis explains:

Why are the authorities so tolerant of a corruption that has penetrated their own ranks? This tolerance--in a regime that is so forthright and ruthless in punishing all other crimes--is due first and foremost to the fact that too high a proportion of the members of the ruling elite is itself involved in the corruption. The proportion is so great that not even the all-powerful Politburo wants to risk a general purge of the ruling elite or the open confrontation with this elite that would result.

Another reason is the regime's fear of destroying a legend that has been built up over sixty years by the propaganda machinery of the Soviet Union and its leadership, made up of chastely honest "servants of the people" whose personal needs are few and modest.[28]

Smith relates an anecdote told by a Russian during his stint in the USSR. It sums up the Russians' understandings of their corruption and their state: "I think," says Ivan to Volodya, "that we have the richest country in the world." "Why?" asks Ivan. "Because for nearly 60 years everyone has been stealing from the state and still there is something left to steal."[29]

NOTES

1   M.D. is a Russian immigrant with insight into the complexities of Soviet life. Her description of the building of this hotel meshed with my observations resulting from a stay at the Cosmos during the fall of 1980. M.D., although a woman with little formal education, possesses the ability to see with a "sociological imagination" and to assess situations with the precision of an artist.

2   Konstantin Simis, USSR: The Corrupt Society (New York: Simon and Shuster, 1982), p. 179.

3   Hedrick Smith, The Russians (New York: Ballantine Books, 1976), p. 108.

4   Harrison Salisbury, A Journey for Our Times (New York: Harper and Row, 1983), p. 239.

5   "Andropov's Economic Dilemma," The New York Times, 9 October 1983, Sec. 6, p. 51.

6   Ibid.

7   Simis, p. 253.

8   Ibid., p. 41.

9   Both Smith, p. 65, and Simis, p. 47, describe this type of corruption as part of ordinary Soviet life.

10   Simis, p. 76.

11   Simis, p. 94.

12   Simis, p. 262.

13   Smith, p. 109.

14   See The New York Times, "Why Russia Can't Grow Grain," 11 January 1981, for further description of the theft of food crops.

15   Robert G. Kaiser, Russia: The People and the Power (New York: Pocket Books 1976), p. 208.

16   Smith, p. 98.

17   Simis, p. 259

18 Smith, p. 117.

19 Ibid.

20 "The Russian's Joy and Anguish of Car Ownership," The New York Times, 22 June 1983, p. 2.

21 Kaiser, p. 138.

22 Simis, p. 34.

23 Simis, p. 52.

24 Simis, p. 168.

25 Sergei Dovlatov, The Compromise (New York: Knopf, 1983).

26 "Andropov's Economic Dilemma," p. 86.

27 Ibid., p. 98.

28 Simis, p. 64.

29 Smith, p. 134.

CHAPTER 2

The Meaning of Crime to the Soviet Citizen

No books about Soviet crime and corruption are published within the country. Indeed, not even within the Western world has any literature on the subject appeared until recently, and then only in limited quantity. In part this is because the Soviet Union has been a closed society, revealing very little of itself either to foreign journalists, or to its own press.[1] Neither foreign visitors nor scholars are permitted to examine the context of criminality within the walls of the Soviet state. Questions by professional criminologists visiting the USSR are answered with contrived examples and propaganda-filled evasions. "Crime statistics are a state secret," Shipler was told by the minister of internal affairs.[2]

"Do you have any juvenile delinquency or children who need detention?" I asked. "Our children listen to their parents," I was told. "They do not get into bad habits like your American children do. I have read about how 'bad' your teenagers are because of your system," an Intourist guide in Leningrad told me. Yet at each bus stop, each place where any foreigners congregate, we were surrounded by boys who at best resembled those from "Our Gang" and at worst were both rough and discomforting.[3]

The attempt to assess the context of criminality in the Soviet system without the aid of those who have spent their time within

Russia itself is difficult. However, as more and more American tourists have been able to enter the USSR, as more and more American companies have stationed technicians within, as the Soviet citizen has through technological advances begun to see more of our world, we in turn have been able, if only in microscopic proportion, to dissect aspects of the Soviet system that until recently have been invisible. In part, this invisibility has been because we too have been victims of the overlying image of contentment projected by the Soviet state. We saw its citizenry as a whole, working doggedly toward a Soviet future. Except for those whom the Soviets label dissidents and dissatisfied Jews, we saw the Soviet citizens in the image created by Soviet press organs.

It is only now, with over 250,000 Jewish immigrants from the Soviet Union, both in the United States and in Israel, and with approximately 20,000 Russian immigrants of other national origins, that some representation of the face of crime within the USSR reaches us.[4] Even though its parameters are still shadowy, we can document the fact that the Soviet system is riddled with both crime and corruption. So vast is the network of illegal activity there that it becomes impossible to separate the culture's operational codes into "legal" and "illegal."

EXPECTANCIES AND UNDERSTANDINGS

Human social relationships are governed through a series of social norms. These norms are standard rules about social understandings and imply what a human being should and should not do in specific circumstances. Behavior can differ, and indeed it will differ, from these norms unless social sanctions are introduced to bring about conformity. These sanctions can be in the form of criminal laws, i.e., formal sanctions. They can also take the form of moral values and other social or personal understandings. Although the latter are not static, they define for us all the proper method of conformance to the norms of both our larger social world and our smaller, subcultural or private social world. For the maintenance of social order, these norms must exist. However, they are not stable, eternal entities but rather in many cases are flexible, shifting series of expectancies, which have been learned through generational cultural transmittal and through personal, social experiences.

Each of us sees our world through a background series of expectancies and these expectancies govern our action and thought. Although norms define social boundaries, they must--like the nucleus of an amoeba--provide some central stability to the ever-changing borders if constancy of social action and social thought is to be communally understood. It is our expectancies that surround our understanding of social norms and provide assurance for us that others will act within anticipated boundaries. Many years ago Ellsworth Faris described these understandings as follows: "We live in a world of 'cultural reality,' and the whole furniture of earth and choir of heaven are to be described and discussed as they are conveyed by men. Caviar is not a delicacy to the General. Cows are not food to the Hindu. Mohammed is not the prophet of God to me. To an atheist, God is not God at all."[5] Only consistency of norms and in turn consistency in social understandings can provide a relatively stable and nonthreatening social world for those within it. In complex modern societies, legal codes become the instruments of definition of behavior that is considered outside the acceptable areas of the given society. These codes attempt to define behavior outside the tolerance limits of societal and group norms and keep the members of a given society in line in order to so control behavior as to ensure, at least in some minimal way, that there will be enough conformity to group expectancies to ensure predictable behavior from most of the society's members.

Toward this end, there are basically two forms of social control. The first might be defined as the "internalization of group norms."[6] Here conformity is brought about through a socialization process where the knowing of what is desirous and the knowing of what is expected brings about a willingness to conform. The second process of social control might be defined as "external pressures in the form of external sanctions from others."[7] It is here that both negative and positive sanctions are employed in order to bring about conformance to the rules of a society. Both informal controls, such as ostracism and gossip, and formal ones, such as legal penalties, are involved in the keeping of the desired behaviors of a particular society in proper channels.

Implicit and explicit understandings play a crucial part in all of this. One must know, not on a hit-or-miss basis, what is generally considered permissible and what is not. Social controls cannot be random if a society is not to develop a schizophrenic overlay. Trust, which allows one to predict the consequences of the behavior of others, at least in some minimal way, is a necessity if those who exist within a given society are able to move about with an understanding of the consequences of their acts. Thus a body of written or unwritten laws, which addresses the issues of permissible behavior and their predictable enforcement, allows in some measure a boundary for the behaviors within a society.

Within the Soviet Union, predictability is difficult to attain. "An independent legal system has no logical place in the Soviet system. Traditionally, every individual and institution in the country has been subject to orders from Moscow; everything is subject to a fix."[8] Indeed, it appears that within the Soviet Union there are two sets of operation laws. They are both in similar ways known to Soviet citizens for their unpredictability and discretionary aspects.

Simis writes about the discrepancy in the governmental system of law and governing. He describes the dual system of government within the country. On one side are the Soviets, the elected councils, which through the Council of Ministers and other administrative agencies are empowered by the constitution to carry out the functions of government. On the other is the Communist party. This, the only legal party in the country, but not even mentioned in the constitution, is the real power, according to Simis: "That power encompasses all spheres of public and private life; it is just as absolute on the national level as it is within each district, each region, and each Union Republic."[9]

Since the state is subject to Party decisions concerning use of all human and economic resources and since the state is the sole employer for the population, there exists within the USSR total Party control of every facet of life:

> All the country's resources--land, water, factories, banks, transport systems, trade and services, educational and scientific establishments; even entertainment--belong to the state, which is to say that they are under the control of the party apparat. That strengthens the Party's control over society as a whole and over each citizen individually, since it turns the Party into a monopoly employer, able to prevent the employment in any job of anyone who fails to observe the unwritten rules on which the Party's power is based.[10]

Simis concludes that legality is not operant in the USSR. The ability of Party officials to supersede all laws, to intercede in court matters, and to violate principles of the constitution willfully precludes any kind of government of laws. In fact, those elected officials who are presumably the agents of government and of the people in fact "can--indeed, must--violate the law on orders from [the] opposite number in the Party apparat."[11]

Soviet leaders intervene in the legal process whenever they feel it necessary. Soviet laws are arbitrary by nature, stemming as they do from desires to increase or decrease adherents to a particular social custom and from momentary revisions of concerns and political needs. Kaiser reports that Russian lawyers within the USSR are more in tune with the Western standard of respect for law than others within the Soviet system. "Respect for the law is one of those Western notions--like fair play or rationalism--which don't find a natural refuge in the Russian character."[12] A traffic policeman can hand a summons to the one he views as a guilty party in a traffic accident and demand a confession of guilty, a signed confession, or payment of a fine on the spot. The concept of legal rights seems to play no part in the legal system in the USSR.

Soviet citizens seem "to see the law as a means to an end-- punishing criminals, preventing undesirable behavior, allocating the blame in a dispute.[13]   Thus, if you view social boundaries as defined by norms that are enforced through various sanctions, the USSR's system would seem to fulfill the expectancies of no one.   The very arbitrary nature of the desires of those within the party to increase or decrease production, open the borders to a wide range of tourists or close them, permit jeans to be bought, or not permit them unless they are of Soviet manufacture, all produce a schizophrenic environment for those who attempt to govern their actions by understandings based on previous experience.

PRIVATE AND PUBLIC CRIMINALS

The concept of a criminal, then, has various meanings for the Soviet citizen.   There are private criminals and public criminals.   One who robs, rapes, or murders is a private criminal[14]: one who has done wrong to another person.   This type of criminal is perhaps better understood in our society than is the public criminal: one who steals, bribes, corrupts, or carries on a private business with state supplies.   In the U.S., the public criminal is viewed as one whom the state sees as criminal but average citizens probably are much less scornful than the state (in its public face) would desire.

The Soviet citizen will condemn criminal activity directed against individuals.   Crimes against the person have a quality that permits universal condemnation.   The other type of crime, that which permeates the USSR because it is "the land of Kleptomania," as Simis describes it, evokes only token social control.[15]   How successful can enforcers of sanctions be if they are involved in the same activities   And if, at any particular moment, it is of interest to crack down on the populace, then it is the final realization of the fear that all Soviet citizens live with, because they are indeed cognizant of the legal violations in which they are involved.

I asked M.D. why some people were involved in legal violations and others were not.   Her reply showed the desperate dilemma confronting many in the USSR:

When Mischa was little we lived in Siberia.   It was a poor life and even milk for him was dear for us.   One day when my husband and my older son went to work I pleaded with them to bring me back a few nails so that I could trade them for some milk for Mischa.   When my husband and son returned, my husband was furious.   He had spotted the boy with the nails, had discovered his mission, and had made him return them.   "We have to be able to sleep at night," he said.   But you have to understand how you can be forced to do these things.   And there is nothing really wrong, a few nails, but the fear--that kept us from doing that.

J.S. tells me that every day the Soviet citizen says, "Is today the day they will come for me?" Those who steal say each morning, "Well, I got through another day okay." She reports that Soviet citizens, in their other actions with the government are never sure of when they are safe. It has been suggested that keeping the general public constantly off guard is an economic measure designed to tighten social control in the USSR. Kaiser has suggested that this is a planned action: that in keeping the populace afraid and cautious, the government keeps their focus of rebellion off the poverty of their lives.[16] Yet my informants seem to feel that the very lack of successful planning in the system precludes this from being a possibility. When questioned about this theory, M.D., a recent immigrant, smiled. "Maybe that is so, but can a government so divided really have such a master plan?" she asked.

In his book, *The Corrupt Society*, Simis discusses the moral decisions involved in Soviet crime. He believes that Soviet citizens are no better and no worse in terms of personal morality than those from elsewhere: there are the good and the bad everywhere. However, he contends that Soviet citizens are aware of the fact that there is a dual system in operation in the USSR. He feels that the quality of Soviet crime is such that the normative boundaries--which need to be maintained for the preservation of order in a society--have broken down.[17] Corruption, secrecy, and theft are now very much a part of the daily life of the Soviet citizen. The ordinary citizen of the USSR is quite aware that the norms vocalized by society are far different from the norms adhered to by that same society. In fact, the socialist society's creed of "to each according to his need" is hardly given allegiance.[18]

Both Kaiser and Shipler point out that lying seems to be an ordinary response among Russians. "Russians find it easy to fib."[19] Both speculate whether this response is the result of situational changes, which, like the proverbial barometer, rises and falls with minute changes in pressure.

Indeed, ordinary citizens in the USSR know that to be honest and truthful, not to participate in the underground economy, and to avoid involvement in the system of corruption, is to create a situation tantamount to total deprivation of both goods and services. They exist in a moral standard that permits morality in private dealings with members of primary groups while excluding morality in dealings with members of secondary groups. In the words of David Shipler:

> This double standard results from the complete alienation of the Soviet individual from governmental power. The Soviet citizen rarely comprehends the totalitarian character of the Soviet regime, rarely recognizes his negative relationship to it. He instinctively responds to material deprivations, to lack of freedom, to the complete corruption of those who rule him,

to the immorality of the regime by excluding everything connected with the state and the economics of the state from the sphere of moral values.

"They"--who rule over us--take bribes, "their trade," "their services" are corrupt through and through, so in dealing with "them" the norms of human morality do not apply. Thus, I might formulate the creed of dual morality.

The virus of corruption, which infects the ruling apparatus of the Soviet Union from top to bottom, is inevitably, by a natural law, spreading to the whole society, to all spheres of its life.[20]

Shipler also describes the fates of those whose sense of right and wrong was particularly clear and whose moves to correct those actions viewed as wrong provoked unusual countermeasures.[21] He details that it is the one who reports illegal actions to superiors whose fate becomes "conversations" with psychiatrists, 10- to 15-day jail sentences, lost jobs, and revoked pensions. These sanctions are employed against the person who seeks to correct a situation of obvious injustice. Transfers to lesser posts, dismissal, harrassment, and threats of psychiatric encounters all follow attempts to object to a system of systematic pilferage, thieving, and the refusal to accept "advice," i.e. veiled suggestions, from the proper "connections."

An interesting phenomenon in the USSR is that a private sanction ceremony has grown in the metropolitan areas. *"Ne kulturno"* (uncultured), the pretty young women strolling arm-in-arm on an Odessa boulevard called to me as I was taking a photo of an empty store shelf. *"Ne kulturno"* the old sea dog barked at the young boys begging for American gum near a departing tour bus. *"Ne kulturno,"* suggested the shop girl to the boys sidling up to us in order to ask about buying our down vests. Everywhere throughout the urban areas where I traveled, Russians chided one another about their public manners.[22]

I speculate that a society that finds itself unable to discern the limitations of criminal and moral behavior has to channel its social-control instruments into plays on manners, exercises in personal power, and personal confrontations. M.S. relates that these habits are so ingrained from her years in the USSR that she finds life in New York almost dangerous. "I stop myself from making public corrections to strangers. 'Tie your shoes.' It is *ne kulturno* to walk that way." Or "Pick up that paper. How can you drop it on the curb like that?' "

Russians cluck about public manners, engaging in constant power plays in their public encounters. They self-correct, engage in a constant ostrich dance of corrective behavior, and enforce a wide variety of informal sanctions throughout their daily personal and public activities.

THE "TOTAL" INSTITUTION

The formal structure of Soviet social control, indeed of the total-ity of the state, rests on a bureaucratic model that has developed many of the characteristics of a total institution. Max Weber's analysis of bureaucracy postulates that it can be technically superior to other forms of organization because it can coordinate a large number of people toward specific objectives. "Precision, speed, unambiguity, knowledge . . . continuity, discretion, strict subordination, reduction of friction and of material and personal costs--these are raised to the optimum point in the strictly bureaucratic administration."[23] Weber saw bureaucracy as having five characteristics that work to further the goals of the organization: specialization, hierarchy of offices, rules and regulations, impartiality, and technical competence. Within the Soviet system's bureaucracy (if in total it fits such a definition), predictability of rules and regulations, by agents of social control who engage in nonimpartiality, and an unclear hierarchy of offices, work to blur the lines of the very goals the system is conceived as having. Although Weber believed that bureaucratic organizations would make good use of available talent, weed out noncontribu-tors, etc., recent research has shown that it is not so.[24] The Soviet system, diverse and enormous as it is, cannot in total be compared to any bureaucratically functioning company or utility as we know it. Certainly there are features, because of size and diversification, that allow comparisons between the actions in the USSR and, for example, those in a public utility company in the United States. Although their outlines will converge at certain points, these examples provide us with little except the factors that make all large organizations (those that are not goal oriented and tightly motivated) somewhat inefficient and totally rule-conscious.[25]

A collateral comparison of the agents of social control in the USSR might be found in Erving Goffman's concept of a total institution in *Asylums*. This type of organization, which deliberately closes out the world, sustains its own internal environment in order to pursue its goals. Goffman sees much of the activity of such institutions, including the army, mental hospitals, and prisons, as being confined to "keeping the lid on." He sees the institution's goals as poorly defined and vast financial and human resources being employed in bureaucratic measures in this pursuit. For Goffman, people in a total institution eventually lose all control over, and all responsibility for, their lives. In the socialization process of living in these places, moral choices are co-opted and the personal sphere of decision making gets smaller and smaller.[26] It is this type of behavior that seems to appear in the daily monitoring of all intrapersonal activities described by my informants. Unable to exercise discretion over many choices within the public sphere, Soviet citizens create areas of private discretion. Involved in bureaucracy, unable to influence most areas of their own life, Soviet citizens become judges of the behavior of others. They evaluate how one should behave in those small measures of life over which they have unthreatened control; pieces of paper thrown down on the street by other ineffectual Soviet citizens allows them some measure of power. Informal social sanctions, mores and modes of behavior, and those understandings that surround them provide some measure of unthreatened behavior and allow for creativity of action. Formal social sanctions, i.e., the criminal boundaries, arouse less creative and less consistent measures in the Russian world.

Who judges who is criminal and when do they so judge? If, as the literature and my informants report, those who carry out criminal acts in the USSR are not the minority of society but are instead the majority, then where are the boundaries and what is the nature of normal behavior? Is criminal behavior for this population then normal behavior? Where are the judges? Inherent in these questions is not only the action judged criminal but also the time and place it is so judged. "The citizen must be immediately nimble or numb to respond appropriately to each shift in the party line, no matter how outrageously it contradicts an earlier line."[27] Under the leadership of Yuri Andropov the attempt to revitalize a sagging economy invoked rules and regulations as well as press announcements of rule enforcement. "The Weekly Law Gazette has announced a sweeping increase in penalties for a wide range of crimes, including harsher punishments for economic misdeeds."[28] These penalties include confiscation of personal possessions of convicted embezzlers and extortionists; exclusion from amnesties of those convicted of pecuniary offenses; requests for letters from workers about bureaucrats defrauding the state; police raids on restaurants, food stores, and cinemas to pick up those who should be, and are not, working; Young Communist League members asked to identify shirkers on construction sites; readers of the Gazette asked to fill out printed questionnaires informing on idleness of fellow workers or managers.

Given the arbitrary nature of these policies and given that those asked to report are already aware that the consequences of this behavior might be more harmful to themselves than to those involved in proscribed activities, the prospect of much correction taking place is negligible. Michael Rusman deals with this concept of social power as follows: In all social systems, prohibitions vary according to the intensity with which they are demanded, the probability of their being sanctioned, and the severity with which they are policed. All these factors may themselves be influenced by the identity and the social location of the violator of specific prohibitions.[29]

It is important when analyzing social systems and their operational legal and moral codes to distinguish between myth systems and operational codes. Myth systems are the rules and understandings that define right and wrong and that have no shadings--that is, their meanings are clear cut. Operational codes tell operators when, by whom, and how specific wrong things may be done. People "know" what behavior is acceptable in their own social setting and what behavior is not. I suggest that the schizophrenic nature, the ever-changing codes in Soviet society, provide the operator with a variety of unclear signals and rationalizations. These provoke behavior that in turn accepts a vast amount of daily criminality as a norm in most groups. Persons develop a way of seeing that permits them to focus on certain things and not to see others.[30] Social judgments do not condemn activity that the state, as the arm of law enforcement, selects (erratically) as in need of social correction.

Thus the value system in the Soviet Union accepts a vast amount of criminality as normal daily behavior. It encourages an ethic that turns a blind eye to stealing, certainly stealing from the state, and that permits a vast amount of daily expression of myth system, far removed from the operational code needed for survival in the system. This then is the underlying aspect of life in the system that is at this point providing us with a large amount of new immigrants.[31]

THE IMMIGRANT FROM THE USSR

Theorists have speculated that the act of emigration is in itself a particular kind of self-selection process. It has been suggested that those who emigrate are those not comfortable in their own environment and/or those who have a will to improve their lot in life. It has also been postulated that there is, indeed, a kind of immigrant personality--one with the determination to succeed. Thus, the Soviet emigrant could be one who has had a determination to take risks even in the USSR. But, as stated, it appears that this kind of risk taking is a "given" of Soviet life. Whether the immigrant who comes to these shores from the Soviet Union was more adept at risk taking or not is of little consequence because that immigrant arrives with a history of having been in some way involved in corruption, if not in outright criminality, in the home country. These immigrants bring with them the internalized subterranean values of their society. They are the products of a complex bureaucratic system and learned behaviors that were needed to circumvent the shortages and administrative dysfunctions of their homeland. They understand their system and how to evaluate situations on a day-to-day basis, cope with hardships, and do their best to survive the very limits of bureaucratic difficulties. They exchange skills on a marginal basis, not in an open, legal, free market; yet they use the Soviet version of free market when necessary. Unlike previous immigrations (and those occurring now from less developed countries) they bring these bureaucratic and manipulative skills with them when they arrive.

In addition, the new immigrants from the USSR come from a technological society. Not only are they skilled in living within bureaucratic systems, but also they have job market abilities that are directly transferrable to the American employment system. They come as housepainters, carpenters, sheet-metal workers, engineers, sewing machine operators, and repairers, manicurists, cosmeticians, various machine operators. Retraining in anything but language is rarely necessary, although it must be noted that lack of language is always a severe limitation. The immigrant intellectual, writer, or artist has always found it difficult to gain entry to established networks and artistic markets. But this immigration provides--in addition to the intellectual--workers who bring useful, comprehensible skills to the job market. These new immigrants then should not be marginal additions to the work world of the United States. They would not seem to need to use illegal means to enter successfully into the society of their new country. The earlier literature about immigration, which saw illegality as a major way in which new Americans could enter social systems, would not seem to apply to these new immigrants, who supposedly come with marketable skills.

But, again unlike 19th- and early 20th-century immigrants, the new immigrants arrive from a social system where beating the system is a normal practice. We can examine how, having grown up in such a society, they use their cultural baggage and how it affects their existence in the United States. It is recognized that all societies, especially advanced bureaucratic ones, have crimes involving circumvention of the bureaucracy's legal procedures. But the cultural understandings of these new immigrants are different in regard to the meaning of crime from those of many other immigrants, so that one must look at this group as unique and as being particularly informative. Can these Russians, having grown up in a culture stressing extralegal anti-bureaucratic mores, shed these mores when they immigrate to a society where these values are less needed?

This new immigration--because of Soviet immigration policies--is primarily a Jewish immigration, though informants have told me that a great number of non-Jews have come in through the same channels. (Some speculate whether these non-Jews are truly immigrants or whether they have arrived with a different purpose.) It is possible to suppose that Jews in the Soviet Union are outside the system and that they are, therefore, engaged in either more or less of the kind of behavior that we have defined as Soviet behavior. One can question whether Jews have ever reached the higher levels of bureaucratic office that provide major access to bureaucratic crime. Salisbury concludes that Stalin's purges of the Jews resulted in less, rather than more, Jewish bureaucratic crime.[32] He sees Jews as precluded more and more from entering the middle and upper levels of bureaucracy, and as having consciously decided not to become involved in situations they define as leading nowhere. Therefore it would appear that in a society where crime is carried out on all levels and especially at the middle level of the bureaucratic structure, Jewish immigrants to these shores may have been limited in terms of access to subtle criminality. Conversely, if it is a fact that these immigrants have not been able to enter the totality of the bureaucratic world, they may have created special criminal channels in which to operate. From my informants, I understand that both situations occur. Some Jews were part of midlevel bureaucracy; others survived by committing illegal acts against it. All my informants seem to agree that the Jews who come here are representative of the total Soviet world. Three generations of life, under the flag of the USSR, have homogenized many of these Jews into Russians. Some have never known their Jewishness except as an item on official papers; others are unable to separate their Russianness and their Jewishness. Law-enforcement sources make clear their desire not to call this problem a Jewish one but rather a criminal one. Their information confirms the speculation by informants as to those already apprehended that their Jewishness is not a factor. For our purposes we are interested more in how this new immigrant group reacts to a culture where previously adaptive criminal values are not necessary for survival.

AMERICAN VS. RUSSIAN UNDERSTANDINGS

Before examining the behavior of these immigrants in the United States, some discussion is necessary about the understanding of crime in this country. Part of American understandings and the openness of discussion in a country bounded by a free press and constitutional guarantees is the concept "Everyone is doing it." In America, beating the system, being particularly clever, circumventing the letter of the law, if not the law itself, is often considered a virtue. Sharp business practices are regarded as part of an American success ethic unless they become linked with extortion, violence, or conviction. Corporate crime is commonplace in the forms of thefts from other companies, and theft of ideas, plans, and planners. Corruption and bribery seem to dominate news articles about police, governmental employees, and political leaders. Not a week goes by without some scandal of major proportion being displayed on our television screens for all to view. "America," said Walter Lippman, "is beginning to accept a new code of ethics that allows for chiselling and lying,"[33] and Mark Twain noted years ago that Congress comprises the only totally American criminal class. Robert Jackall, writing about bureaucratization of the economy, concludes, "Bureaucracy . . . breaks apart substance from appearance, action from responsibility, and language from meaning. . . .[It] erodes internal and even external standards of morality."[34]

Concern with the loss of American values is at the forefront of every political campaign, every neighborhood gathering, every church occasion. Americans are as concerned with what they see as their declining morality as they are involved with "making it." Yet symbolically, no matter how violated our legal system becomes, the fundamental difference between the meaning of crime in the USSR and the meaning of crime in the United States is that we circumscribe our behaviors and attempt to govern our morality under the concept that this is a nation of laws. Robert Bellah sees America as operating under a set of national beliefs that bind the citizenry together. He sees Americans as having a general system of belief in a God (of civil origin) who is universal rather than sectarian and who is not as concerned with personal ends as with law, justice, order, and other matters of interest to the entire community.[35]

It is a central fact of the social order of America that we are engrossed, both as citizens and as sociologists, in a constant examination and reassessment of the least defined boundaries of legal and extralegal behavior. Indeed, American sociologists and criminologists take turns in accusing the society of which they are a part of deviant behaviors that they see as peculiarly American. Edwin Schur sees our crime as but a reflection of a society that is, by its very nature, criminal.[36] Charles Silberman looks to violence as a trait that is "[as] American as Jesse James," a trait that is culturally reinforced through literature and myth."[37] Indeed, literature reflects the very nature of the American, as still engaged in the pursuit described by de Tocqueville as the essence of being American, the pursuit of morality and equality. No other society examines itself or attempts to reform itself in quite the same way as we do. It is this very attitude of the acceptance by the community of a sense of morality that distinguishes our society from that of the Soviet Union.[38]

Additionally, our midlevel bureaucrats, middle-management executives, midlevel factory operators are those whose system beating, when it occurs, tends to be most minimal. Higher levels of criminal activity can be pinpointed to upper-level corporate executives, or lower-class and under-class society members. Indeed, though the popular dictum gloomily decrees that "everyone is doing it," in effect most would agree that the criminal here is part of the minority rather than the majority of the population. From all available literature about the USSR, this is not so there:

there they are all (or almost all) voluntarily or involuntarily "doing it" to some extent.

Part of the very spirit of American government is the constant attempt to clean up crime. Commission after commission has been formed to detect and then prosecute those who violate the moral system as ascertained by the American ethic. Nothing is more popular than this battle between good and evil. It has almost taken on the air of a spectator sport. Witness the concept of "entrapment," where we warn enforcers not to create the very crimes they want to uncover. Certainly many in the bureaucratic system of our governmental lodges partake of forbidden fruit, but many do not. In the USSR not doing is tantamount to exclusion from the social order.

In addition, the organization within which one can behave corruptly here in the United States is not in operation for a 24-hour day. Here, organizational corruption is but one limited part of the total scheme of life, for although one's social network is often centered around job-related persons, the neighborhood, the school, and the sports field intervene to prevent the totality of corruption for most individuals. In the USSR, all of these criminal activities are primed, their very equipment and habitats greased, by the need for universal corruption.

Several of my informants have discussed how "boring" their life here in the United States has become and even how disturbed their domestic existence is. They report that in the USSR their very raison d'etre was the ability to cast out into the water of criminality and return with that extra pair of gloves, that morsel of meat or fish. Here was the excitement of daily life, now unattainable. Here were the heros made: "My husband could always provide extras," said S.R., "but here all I ask from him is that he bring home money. I can provide right in the local stores. It hurts our marriage and takes away the excitement."

In addition, one can, and indeed many in the United States do, live one's whole life untouched by the criminality involved in bureaucratic maneuvering, thefts of services or goods, or violation of criminal penalties. We point quickly to the welfare cheater, the Medicaid defrauder, the cop on the take. And indeed these criminals in the bureaucratic networks do exist and operate quite blatantly without the fear that is so dominant in the life of the Soviet citizen. This is but a small percentage of a population who are able to live their entire lives untouched by the total criminality inherent in Soviet life. The existence there, the housing, food, clothes, travel, jobs--the very meat of daily living--cannot be attained on the salaries provided for such things. This is the understanding of the citizenry. This totality of daily living can only be achieved through extralegal means and connections.

J.S. proposes that shortages become an engrossing factor of living and thus preclude the general Russian population from focusing on matters of political and human concern. She sees this as purposeful governmental policy aimed at distracting the public:

> It is why the dissidents are such a thorn. They don't care if they have a meal or an extra sweater. They bother themselves with larger issues and then the government has to take issue with them and this causes problems. But the rest of the people are too busy trying to eat and live to worry about anything else. And it is public policy by the government to continue this.

It is of interest to discover whether, when barriers to economic producion are removed, when the immigrant can participate in an economic free market, the common-sense world of cultural learnings acquired through years of socialization in Soviet society will be thrust off. Pavel Litvinov has suggested that those who come from the USSR tend to bring totalitarian solutions to the problems of their new land. One wonders whether the solutions they have brought are also nonlegal and corrupt.[39]

NOTES

1 For a first hand account about creating news within the Soviet Union see Dovlatov, (1983). In addition, Smith, Kaiser and Shipler also discuss the secrecy inherent in Soviet dealings with the press.

2 Shipler, p. 230.

3 Shipler has a useful discussion about juvenile crime within the USSR; pp. 226-234, pp. 236-237, pp. 239-245.

4 See Soviet Jewish Affairs, Vol. 12, No. 3, 1982.

5 Ellsworth Faris, The Nature of Human Nature (New York: McGraw-Hill, 1937), pp. 150-151.

6 See John Finley Scott, The Internalization of Norms (Englewood Cliffs, N.Y.: Prentice-Hall, 1971)

7 Ibid.

8 Kaiser, p. 163.

9 Simis, p. 24.

10 Simis, pp. 26-27.

11 Ibid.

12 Kaiser, p. 164.

13 Ibid.

14 Reports about violent crimes in the USSR are just that, reports. There are no available crime statistics but murder and crimes of violence have been reported to outsiders and are mentioned frequently in the Soviet press.

15 Simis, p. 248.

16 Kaiser, pp. 342-387.

17 Simis, p. 298.

18   An interview with D.R., a recent immigrant and a lawyer who practiced in the higher reaches of the Soviet court system, confirms Simis' contention that those within the USSR are engaged in a dual moral system.

19   Kaiser, p. 268, and Shipler, p. 245.

20   Simis, p. 298.

21   Shipler describes how hypocrisy is learned within the USSR (pp. 113-118) and how it is practiced (pp. 223-248) in a state of what he calls "moral weightlessness."

22   Shipler, pp. 55-56 describes this conduct as an exercise in power by the powerless.

23   From Max Weber: Essays in Sociology, trans. and ed. H.H. Gerth and C. Wright Mills (New York: Oxford University Press, 1946).

24   Peter M. Blau and Marshall W. Meyer, Bureaucracy in Modern Society 2d ed. (New York: Random House, 1971).

25   See William J. Goode, "The Protection of the Inept," American Sociological Review, Vol. 32 (February 1967), pp. 5-19.

26   Erving Goffman, Asylums (New York: Doubleday, 1961).

27   Joseph Bensman and Bernard Rosenberg, Mass, Class and Bureaucracy, (Englewood Cliffs, New Jersey: Prentice-Hall, 1963), p. 278.

28   "The Emergence of Andropov," The New York Times 27 February 1983, p. 24.

29   Michael W. Reisman, Folded Lies (New York: The Free Press, 1979).

30   A full discussion of this concept can be found in Karl Mannheim, Freedom, Power and Democratic Planning (London: Routledge and Kegan Paul, 1968).

31   In actuality these persons are technically immigrants since they do not come in under a quota, but rather as political refugees.

32   Salisbury, p. 319.

33 Margaret Halsey, The Corrupted Giant (London: MacDonald and Co., 1968).

34 Robert Jackall, "Moral Mazes, Bureaucracy and Managerial Work" unpublished article, 1982.

35 Robert Bellah, Beyond Belief (New York: Harper and Row, 1970).

36 Edwin M. Schur, Our Criminal Society (Englewood Cliffs, New Jersey: Prentice-Hall, 1969).

37 Silberman, p. 21-47.

38 See Edmund Cahn The Moral Decision (Bloomington: Indiana University Press, 1956), and Jerome Frank Courts on Trial (New York: Athenaeum, 1963).

39 "Lives of 2 Soviet Families Here," The New York Times, 4 September 1977.

CHAPTER 3

Sociology and the Immigrant

On March 27, 1953, the world greeted with both joy and relief the announcement that the threat, the fear, the hysteria caused by the dread words *infantile paralysis* could be ended. Jonas E. Salk, in a major medical breakthrough, had not only identified a problem and recognized its devastating effects, but had also isolated its cause and presented a solution through empirical medical research. After years of fear and hysteria about a particular problem affecting humankind, researchers had found a yearned-for solution. Would that the academic world surrounding the field of criminology could duplicate this feat, one so often performed by the academic world surrounding the field of medicine! Yet even to suggest that this could be possible is to evoke a smile on the face of the reader. The academic world surrounding the field of criminal behavior--indeed, surrounding the field of human behavior--has spurred industries, created literature so vast as to fill whole wings of libraries, and has supported, at least in some fashion, legions of academicians, editors, philosophers, and practitioners. Unfortunately, it seems that no matter how dedicated to the pursuit of solutions American criminologists are, the best that they can devise are recommendations for further study of a topic that has proved to be multidimensional.

There are as many theories of criminal behavior as there are kinds of criminality. Emile Durkheim dominated much of sociological thinking and indeed sociology itself, throughout his life and thereafter. Durkheim's description of the processes through which society moves as it becomes more complex--that is, as it moves from the more primitive, "mechanical" society into its more advanced form, the "organic" society,--underlies much sociological thinking even today.[1] In self-sufficient societies whose members hold similar values and do similar work, i.e., in mechanical societies, social cohesion exists. Durkheim sees only a few people in this type of society as having specialized roles. The rest do as they must, not depending on individual initiative or talent.

Durkheim contrasts this with organic society, where there is a specialized and organized division of labor. Writing at a time when the world was in the midst of great turmoil, where the French Revolution and rapid industrialization had created among the thinkers of the day a feeling that their world had taken a massive turn into a frightening and industrialized unknown, he saw every society as moving along a continuum from the mechanical to the organic. He saw law playing different roles in each type of society. In the mechanical society law was a means of regulating norms and keeping members of the group from deviating too greatly. He stressed that in the organic society law purposefully restrained wrongful acts between the various parts of the society, as opposed to the members within, and provided a means for settlement of intergroup grievances.[2] Durkheim saw, as a primary force making for social solidarity within the mechanical society, the small groups who are unable to fulfill the collective goals of their society and who therefore, by being punished, act as a unifying force for the rest of the society. In their violation of the collective conscience of their society, and in being punished, they provide it with a force for solidarity. Indeed, Durkheim saw crime as normal within society and maintained that if behaviors now classified as criminal were all to become normatively permissible, a society would have to define other behaviors as criminal. He felt that this is so not because the inherent nature of human beings is bad, but rather because without such behaviors the society would be too repressive for any social change.

Emile Durkheim maintained that society needs criminality in order to maintain boundaries on permissible behavior.[3] He felt that behavior labeled criminal is not necessarily pathological but rather that society itself imposes distinctions on various types of behavior in order to define the norms of the society. Since he saw human appetites as insatiable, he postulated that if acts now considered crimes were in some fashion curtailed, then people would commit acts of a less deviant nature and these would then be elevated to the status of crimes. He saw such a process as a never-ending one of definition.

Following his premise of insatiability, Durkheim concluded that society has to establish social order in order to control these appetites. Having done so, it also provides opportunities for those who cannot fulfill their goals within a social order set by the society. He postulated that collective order breaks down when there are great swings in the economic practices of a society. Although Durkeim's theories of anomie were not primarily concerned with criminality, he saw economic pressures in Western society as pushing individuals toward individualism and hence suicide when they could not define or achieve their imagined goals.

Primary among those who follow Durkheim's reasoning is Robert Merton. Although he says he does not deal with individual motivational forces, Merton nevertheless emphasizes the social goals that exert pressure "upon certain persons in a society to engage in non-conformist rather than conformist conduct."[4] In a footnote, he mentions that the psychoanalytic approach to crime and its causation is a variation of the concept of original sin. His own approach may well be called a doctrine of "socially derived sin."

Merton divides social structure into two aspects: the first is culturally defined goals, purposes, and interests--what he terms "aspirational references," and the second is the controls defined by the particular culture of which any individual is a part--what Merton terms "institutional norms." Satisfactions, Merton states, "accrue to individuals who conform to both constraints. . . . Success is reckoned in terms of the product and in terms of the process, in terms of the outcome and in terms of activities. Continuing satisfactions must derive from sheer participation in a competitive order as well as from eclipsing one's competitors if the order itself is to be sustained.[5] However, if the satisfaction that accrues from the ability to achieve culturally defined goals through in-stitutionally approved means is lacking, or if such attainment is impossible, then Merton confronts us with the concept of "socially derived sin" by suggesting that what he terms "aberrant conduct" occurs. He sees this type of conduct as part of the process of dissociation--where one removes one's activity from the sphere of culturally defined aspirations and socially structured means.

Looking at American society, Merton sees people as products not only of their ability or inability to achieve wealth (which he sees as the basic tenet to success here), but also of what he terms "biological drives," which break though societal restraints. There-fore, Americans are not only swept through society by forces that display vast areas of success possibilities with which they have few legitimate avenues but in addition they have the added burden of a whole background of biology. Merton defines for us that it is most difficult for people to face failure in a society that places a high premium on economic affluence and social ascent for all its members:

> Our egalitarian ideology denies by implication the existence of noncompeting groups and individuals in pursuit of pecuniary success. The same body of success symbols is held desirable for all. These goals are held to transcend class lines...
> The American stress on pecuniary success and ambitiousness for all thus invites exaggerated anxieties, hostilities, neuroses, and antisocial behavior.
> This theoretical analysis may go far toward explaining the varying correlations between crime and poverty.[6]

Thus Merton stresses that we are tossed around by social pressures to achieve that which society has told us are our symbols of success, and if we are denied the avenues to travel toward those structures of societal pleasure, we will use the byways of circumvention to get to the same end. We will revert in some way to biological fighting and will attempt to use crime, vice, and fraud in order to achieve economic success. If neither method works for us, we will opt out. We may then people the sidewalks and streets as no-longer-caring dropouts. We may even revert to the hordes of the great unwashed in order just to be. Merton, writing in the egalitarian spirit of the 1930s, concluded that our cultural system pushes us to strive for certain goals that are normatively regulated. He stressed that there are class-linked patterns of socialization and saw those who respond or fail to respond to society's goals as having different socializations and thus different adaptations.

These two theoretical perspectives, although they are related, view crime from different angles. Durkheim saw criminality as a natural feature of any society. Merton saw American society with its success goals as fostering deviant behavior that takes various forms and is therefore difficult to predict. Merton's view of crime is of interest because it presents us with the question of boundaries of socially permitted behavior and allows us to ask if his anomie theory accounts for all sorts of deviance or just some kinds. Does this theory have a place in the movements of a population from a society with one set of boundaries to one with another? How do immigrants fit into this type of theory, and how does this concept of anomie fit in with the writings of criminologists who see American values as less clear than apparently Merton does?

Both Durkheim and Merton deal with crime as a factor of society that is already in place and that has value systems unaltered by the addition of new members to the population. To them, society's members are either able or unable to cope with the value systems of their given society and with the social changes that take place as time and growth occur in that society. However, American society has become the recipient of populations bringing with them value systems from other established social orders. These populations have grown up within the means-and-end setting of one social system and have to assimilate both in the process of social change. Of interest to us is just how people who come into a society affect that society and how they, in turn, are affected by that society.

Much of the literature about the immigrant and crime suggests that the immigrant, unable to achieve success within the society, uses marginal means to move up the social ladder. These marginal means are suggested as a way for people from another country to enter the social system of the nation into which they have newly immigrated. Somehow there is always the assumption that criminality begins with immigration, that it results from attempts to enter the mainstream of life within the new country and the realization that this is impossible. These concepts presuppose that new immigrants (or their children), unable to speak the language and ignorant of the mores and structures of their new country, can consciously find a marginal and often criminal means for entry into the economic and social world of America.

Background contingencies of the new immigrant population must be examined before one can comfortably adapt these various theoretical perspectives to the study of new immigrants. The concept of criminality in a society as a means of social change, the belief that crime is normal in societies, and the concept of marginality as a means of entering a social order must be reexamined against the background of the particular new immigrant groups entering the United States.

Sociological literature reflects the belief that the immigrant discovered crime upon immigration. Only with Italian immigrants is there some suggestion that their previous status reflected the kind of behavior engaged in by some of these immigrants before they arrived in the United States. Italian immigrants, particularly from Southern Italy, came from a semifeudal society, where they had little or no respect for governmental laws and took upon themselves the creation of an alternative, illegal social order. This population is responsible for a wide body of literature linking it to a criminal structure that dominated substantial aspects of both the political and the criminal structure of their host societies for many years.

CRIME AND THE SLUM: CULTURAL LEARNINGS

Much of the literature about the nature of crime in America dates to the early days of American sociology and coincides with the beginning of the largest wave of immigrants to reach these shores (1890-1924). It is therefore not surprising that early criminology--indeed, early sociology--looked to the issues of the day and focused at first on the formidable social problems encountered--crime, urbanization, cultural and ethnic boundaries--and generally reflected the concerns of a nation engrossed in the absorption of a newly arrived immigrant population.

Sociologists of the day, concerned with the problems of urbanization and crime, looked at this new immigrant as someone who had to be socialized to proper white Anglo-Saxon mores. Sociologists, legislators, police, and the institutions that dealt with new immigrants hoped to resocialize them in order to integrate them with the white Anglo-Saxon superstructure of American society.[7] The immigrants stood out: they looked different; they acted differently; their actions were suspect even if they were not criminal. Even their characteristic patterns of crime were different.

In *World of Our Fathers,* Irving Howe reports that delinquency among new Eastern European immigrants at the turn of the century, forced governmental authorities to fund reformatories for Jewish children who had gotten into trouble with the law.[8] He details the problem of youths committing misdemeanors as so great that the City of New York provided $110 per child annually for correctional institutions. "A similar arrangement was already in effect within the Protestant and Catholic communities. . . . [The] magnitude of this problem [was so large] that the Protectory Movement had to continue its work through and beyond the First World War."[9] Yet we are talking about immigrant children and their misdemeanors. One wonders whether the society of church-going and work-ethic-oriented Americans selected for containment those who were now so visible because their numbers were so large that they could not be ignored. Those selected were different, foreign, unattractive, and often dirty. Indeed, it has been suggested that with the onset of the Industrial Revolution, women of rank and consequence found work in a wide variety of activities that were not economically profitable but allowed them to enter a world of reformation. There they could nurture those residing in slums, prison, and various charitable institutions.[10] So American society was at a crossroads of opportunity: we had native American socializers and those who needed socializing. Teaching, learning theory, and the new immigrant all provided the means for theory creation by a burgeoning number of academics involved in the new area of Social Science.

Yet slums and ghettos have always existed. Throughout centuries there was a general conviction that those in the lower class produced little. Merton's concept of those who had different socialization seems to agree with this notion. The gap between rich and poor seemed natural and inevitable. Slum living and those who had lived in slum conditions were written off as poor because of God's will. Although occasionally philanthropic endeavors were carried out as a result of Christian duty, for the most part it was not until after the Industrial Revolution that White Anglo-Saxon society began to feel that those crowded together in slums must be taught and reformed. Indeed, a federal government report in 1894 described those who inhabited slums as "squalid and criminal."[11] The milieu for crime and delinquency has existed in slums through centuries and throughout cultures.[12] In America, the study of these conditions grew largely with the study of sociology.

Yet there is nothing about these understandings that refutes the literature of Dickens and others who looked to areas of crowding as breeders of blight, conventional crime, prostitution, illegitimacy, infant mortality, and high rates of death and disease. There are arguments to be made about the fact that the residents of such areas appear suspect to police and often are defined as suspect in such fashion as to feel that they are indeed different.[13] However, there is ample support for the conclusion that cultural learnings in areas of such disorganization favor crime and various other behaviors socially unacceptable to the upper classes. One must not only look to situational factors favoring criminal behavior but also must integrate those factors into a more complex formulation, including familiar influences and societal responses. Certainly the need to anglicize a population that did not adhere to "standard" American motivations and behaviors--even though they had remained unnoticed by the general American population--is apparent in much of the literature about slum life until the Industrial Revolution and the mass immigration of European peasants in new urban slums.

Marshall B. Clinard and Robert F. Meier have devoted much scholarship to the analysis of slums. They maintain that the slum is a unique place with an inbred culture.

> The slum has a culture of its own. The slum way of life is learned, and passes from generation to generation, in the process developing rationale, structure, and even defense mechanisms which provide means of continuation in spite of deprivations and difficulties. While all slum residents are influenced in some degree by this slum culture, all do not become a real part of it.[14]

The study of crime and the criminal has focused on behavior in a slum and on criminality in slum areas for two diverse reasons. The first, because the type of crime within the slum is readily visible to enforcers of the law: that is, it is overt. Slum living in many instances is, as a result of the very conditions which are slumlike (crowding, noise, overpopulation, poverty), a tableau of life in public places and thus visible to all. Elliot Lebow, in

Tally's Corner, vividly depicts how we evaluate slums by our impressions of the apparent idleness of their inhabitants.[15] Irving Piliavin and Carl Werthman, in their chapter on "Gang Members and Ecological Conflict" in *Juvenile Delinquency,* illustrate just how law enforcers look upon the ghetto scene:

> From the front seat of a moving patrol car, street life in a typical Negro ghetto is perceived as an uninterrupted sequence of suspicious scenes. Every well dressed man or woman standing aimlessly on the street during hours when most people are at work is carefully scrutinized for signs of an illegal source of income; every boy wearing boots, black pants, long hair, and a club jacket is viewed as potentially responsible for some item on the list of muggings, broken windows, and petty thefts that still remain to be cleared; and every hostile glance directed at the passing patrolman is read as a sign of possible guilt.[16]

The second reason that the study of crime and the criminal focused particularly on slum areas was that the population of such areas presented a culture different from that of lawmakers and middle-class Americans. In dealing with ghetto crime, we have to acknowledge that the sociologist was so immersed in the behavior of the criminal, he often forgot to view himself as an observer. Immigrant crime, slum crime, and the crimes of the poor present a visible, studiable diorama upon which to fashion theories of criminality. However, observers always measure that diorama against the real-life scenario of their own background.

CRIME AND LEARNED BEHAVIOR

Edwin H. Sutherland's theory of differential association argues that social changes brought about by the Industrial Revolution produce conditions favorable to criminality.[17] He postulates that a criminal act occurs when a situation appropriate for it is present. Basically, Sutherland developed learning theory for application to criminal behavior, i.e., behavior that violates the observed social codes of a particular society. He took one individual and placed him in a situation that provided him with reinforced learning experiences, and then concluded that crime is learned through such reinforced experiences in association with others who are teachers of these behaviors. He concluded that crime is learned when favorable definitions outweigh unfavorable ones. In effect, if a person whom we shall call "Joe" is brought up in a neighborhood where the big man on the block is the pimp, and this man is engaged in activities that Joe sees as ordinary and productive, then Joe will also see the rewards of these activities, not from the vantage point of the larger society but from the vantage point of a student who can learn, by association with a mentor, patterns necessary for the commission of a crime. Sutherland pointedly asserted, "while criminal behavior is an expression of general needs and values, it is not explained by those general needs and values."[18]

Adding up individual Joes, Sutherland then deals with crime figures and crime facts. Unlike those who are much more impersonal in their theoretical approach either to crime or to the criminal, he pointedly explains that "the crime rate is a summary statement of the number of persons in the group who commit crimes and the frequency with which they commit crimes."[19] Social disorganization, he states, although not a fully satisfactory term, allows us to look to those communities, neighborhoods, environments, where the types of learning favorable to the commission of crime are relatively greater than those in other communities.

This concept of social disorganization gained great favor in early sociology and criminology because of the quality of life in urban areas of the country. Not surprisingly, the influx to this country of various immigrant groups spurred much literature concerning the failure of existing social codes to control those populations who had settled in overcrowded and inadequate housing and who tended to make up the very "summary statement" about crime and criminals of which Sutherland wrote. Indeed, if one added up the total of those who had broken social rules within an urban ghetto neighborhood and compared it with the total of those who had done the same in other areas of the city, one would find both crime rates and social disorganization of larger proportion in the former. Thomas and Znaniecki in *The Polish Peasant in Europe and America* also saw that failure to follow existing social rules ultimately resulted in social disorganization.[20]

Thus, Sutherland's concept of differential association was used to explain not only how one person, our "Joe," became a part of those who lean toward criminal or socially unacceptable behavior, but also how acts that were not a part of the American social tradition were committed. Both Clifford Shaw, writing in *Delinquency Areas* in 1929,[21] and Edwin Sutherland, writing in 1939,[22] saw the expansion of industry and business, the immigration to this country of a variety of immigrant populations, growth, cultural diversity, and various intranational migrations as weakening traditional American forms of social control and, in turn, allowing for high rates of antisocial acts. Since Sutherland also felt that this type of disorganization teaches those who live in such areas to violate social codes, in effect he saw cultural traditions arise that would favor violation of existing codes rather than adherence to them. Though circular in reasoning, this approach to crime does in some fashion establish a relationship of social conditions to crime and delinquency rates. Sutherland's concept of cultural traditions arising in slum situations was never applied to cultural traditions imported from abroad.

Since by definition both crime and delinquency violate the social norms of the society, we are faced with the problem again of confronting Joe and trying to discover how he made his personal choice between adherence and nonadherence to social norms. Somewhere in that same area and within those same non-code-reinforcement areas are those who behaved in more traditional, non-criminal arenas of action.

CRIME AND THE IMMIGRANT: CULTURAL INTERPRETATIONS

Donald Cressey, in an article about Sutherland's theory, explains its current interpretation as follows:

> The current statement of the theory of differential holds, in essence, that "criminal behavior is learned in interaction with persons in a pattern of communication," and that the specific direction of motives, drives, rationalizations, and attitudes--whether in the direction of anti-criminality or criminality--is learned from persons who define the codes as rules to be observed and from persons whose attitudes are favorable to violation of legal codes. . . .
>
> When this idea is applied to a nation, a city, or a group, it becomes a sociological theory, rather than a social-psychological theory. . . . The important general point is that in a multi-group type of social organization, alternative and inconsistent standards of conduct are possessed by various groups, so that individuals who are members of one group have a higher probability of learning to use legal means for achieving success, or of learning to deny the importance of success, while individuals in other groups learn to accept the importance of success and to achieve it by illegal means. Stated in another way, *there are alternative educational processes in operation,* varying with groups, so that a person may be educated in either conventional or criminal means of achieving success.[23] (Italics mine)

In explaining Sutherland's theory, Cressey also accepts Merton's. In order to achieve success within those definitions provided by society, one responds, as a result of an educational process, by behavior that is either law abiding or law violating. The boundaries between are defined at all times by the "ideal" vision of any given society.

Sutherland's learning theory proved particularly appealing to a society that felt that some of its members needed to be resocialized into a value system more in conformity with the American ethic.[24] The immigrant thus provided sociology in America with issues and social problems upon which to build theory. Crime, urbanization, cultural and ethnic boundaries were all reflected in the theoretical writings of a nation engrossed in the absorption of a newly arrived population.

The new urban immigrants (1890-1924) came from the lands of Southern and Eastern Europe--Italy, Greece, Austria-Hungary, Serbia, Romania, Russian Poland, and Russia. They differed from the "old immigrants," who had arrived when the frontier was still open. Those early arrivals on the American frontier had traditions and customs similar to those of prior American settlers. With origins in Northern and Western Europe, they reflected in manner and belief the population already in place.

The new wave of immigrants was a far different population. They were the tired, the poor, the "huddled masses yearning to breathe free" about whom Emma Lazarus wrote. Their problems, coming together with urbanization, provided white Anglo-Saxon American and sociology in particular, with an engrossing learning laboratory. Park's "Human Migration and the Marginal Man,"[25] Thrasher, Shaw, and McKay's studies of slums and crimes in cross-cultural situations,[26] Myrdal's *American Dilemma*,[27] and Cooley's studies on social organizations[28] all exemplify an American social science gaining perspectives from analysis of a new immigrant population.

As C. Wright Mills reminds us in *The Sociological Imagination,* "Every society holds images of its own nature--in particular, images and slogans that justify its system of power and the ways of the powerful. The images and ideas produced by social scientists may or may not be consistent with these prevailing images, but they always carry implications for them."[29] Surely the actors involved in the resocialization of the American immigrant saw their task as glorious. No recognition was afforded to the legitimacy of the alternate life-style of the new American population.

AMERICAN VALUES AND THE IMMIGRANT

Daniel Bell, in "Crime as an American Way of Life," suggests that "Americans have had an extraordinary talent for compromise in politics and extremism in morality."[30] Indeed, the concept that morality is at the very underpinning of American society can be supported by this nation's constant drive on corruption and criminality in an ever increasing ritual of self-criticism. Lexow, Seabury, Kefauver, Watergate, and Koreagate all point to American's demonstrated love for what Edmund Cahn calls "the moral decision." Cahn has said, "Our reaction to an act of moral wrong is a blend of reason that recognizes, of emotion that evaluates, and of glands that pump physical preparation for action."[31] Bell and Cahn both see Americans as having a sense of morality that rises to situational moments and that reflects the Puritan values upon which this country was founded. Bell discusses America's tradition:

> Some truth may lie in Svend Ranulf's generalization that moral indignation is a peculiar fact of middle class psychology and represents a disguised form of repressed envy. The larger truth lies perhaps in the brawling nature of American development and the social character of crime. Crime, in many ways is a Coney Island mirror, caricaturing the morals and manners of a society. The jungle quality of the American business community, particularly at the turn of the century, was reflected in the mode of "business" practiced by the coarse gangster elements, most of them from immigrant families, who were "getting ahead," just as Horatio Alger had urged. In the older, Protestant tradition the intense acquisitiveness . . . was rationalized by a compulsive moral fervor.[32]

Milton L. Barron, writing in *Current Perspectives on Criminal Behavior,* suggests that the same American values that underpin legitimate American life also encourage norm-violating and illegal behavior. Primary among these values is success. Barron quotes professional football's coach Vince Lombardi's advice, "Winning isn't everything, it is the only thing" as a major value of American life. Asserting one's self and succeeding, says Barron, cause those who realize that they will not succeed in legitimate ways to turn to crime and delinquency to achieve their goal.[33]

Additionally, Barron lists "status and power ascendance" in the form of high grades, expensive cars, jewelry, and the understanding that money provides power as a motivating force in criminal behavior. In his criminogenic theory, "toughness," "resistance to authority," "dupery" (P. T. Barnum's observation that a sucker is born every minute), and a dynamic culture with rapidly changing norms contribute to the weakening of the difference between right and wrong.

Bell sees that these desires were satisfied in extralegal fashion by an immigrant population using marginal means for social advancement. He suggests that, unable to achieve their learned American goals through socially acceptable means, they used "crime . . . the illicit activity organized for continuing profit rather than individual illegal acts [as] one of the queer ladders of social mobility in American life."[34] It is difficult to imagine how an immigrant population housed in ghetto conditions was able to interpret the goals of American society so quickly and then to innovate in an attempt to achieve these goals.

Following Bell's concept of ethnic criminal succession, Francis Ianni predicts newer criminal populations following those already established, and includes the black population within this succession, although theirs is hardly a conventional immigrant population. Ianni structures a criminal world of succeeding immigrant populations who dominate organized crime, ending with the supposition that the Italians are leaving organized crime and the Blacks and Puerto Ricans are taking over.[35] He postulates that ethnic groups move in and out of organized crime while the crime, as an American institution, persists.

He sees the new immigrant, unable to achieve success through legitimate means, resorting to marginality. It falls to such immigrants to provide American society with those illicit goods and services that society does not allow to be provided legitimately--gambling, prostitution, drugs, stolen goods, etc. Ianni sees complicity on the part of the various legitimate institutions within society--the police and the politicians--as participating in this illegality through provision of immunity from prosecution. Addressing the question of the new immigrants from Cuba, Ianni sees them as most like the Italian Americans in that: (1) they have structures and cohesive groups that replace other immigrant groups in the ethnic succession of criminality, and (2) they use marginality as entrance into the world of America's legitimate social structure.

In his book *Criminal Justice, Criminal Violence,* Charles Silberman wrote: "American crime is an outgrowth of the greatest strengths and virtues of American society--its openness, its ethos of equality, its heterogeneity--as well as of its greatest vices."[36] Acknowledging that a frontier mentality has permeated American consciousness and that "the metaphors of the West retain their curious hold on the American imagination,"[37] Silberman sees the frontier ethos as having a major role in American culture with "one consequence . . . a general failure to relate means to ends."[38]

These factors were already a part of the American tradition before the wave of new Eastern European immigrants peopled the ghettos; criminality already existed on the American scene, but its face before had been somehow acceptably American. The literature seems to reflect an American awakening to crime at precisely the time of our largest wave of different--that is, non-Anglo-Saxon--immigrants.

As American society moved toward an industrial society, the nature of American crime moved with it. After World War I, prohibition brought big business into the area of providing services to those who wanted something beyond the law. According to Bell, gambling underwent a transition similar to that undergone by business itself, and became a far-reaching corporate enterprise for which levels of success, organization, and leadership paralleled those of legitimate corporate businesses. The illegitimate industries providing criminal services had at their helm men whose similarity to captains of industry was obvious. Although their personal profiles were hardly of the white Anglo-Saxon Protestant makeup, these figures exemplified the very virtues that Americans had grown to respect. They were self-made men who took opportunities when they saw them, organized efficient, profitable enterprises, and saw major organizational growth as a result of planning and competition. Rackets assumed the role of providing services that legitimate enterprises did not want to provide.[39]

These new leaders of an organized criminal industry were largely of Italian origin. Their tight-knit family structure, imported from a Southern Italian society with little respect for government and national law, enabled them to conduct business with supportive and protective allies at their sides. The various families constituting the original Italian Mafia, with their intermarriages and liaisons, created a far-reaching criminal structure that operated, in the first generation, completely outside the law. Bell's theory of marginality seems to have left out the significant factor that some members of this population had come to these shores with a culture conducive to criminal activities already in place. The immigrant criminals had imported values, loyalties, and codes. They chose to exercise these in marginal business here in the United States probably only because that was what they knew how to do.

This population and a newly industrialized country created opportunities for a whole new area of criminality. As more and more people moved into faceless, non-owner-operated businesses, both the increase in organized criminal syndicates and the study of these groups became major focuses of sociological discussion. Fundamental supply services for prostitution, pornography, and narcotics were observed to have structures paralleling general business organizations.[40] General business organizations, in turn, were observed to have structures favoring minimal adherence to legal codes wherever possible.[41] Executive officers of corporations, functioning in the very finest of traditions (at least in the terms defined by Vince Lombardi) were moving to violations of law, which, although not comparable with personal violence in the view of criminal prosecutors, nevertheless defined a new moral violation of the trust of the nation.

In a 1967 report issued by the President's Commission on Law Enforcement and Administration of Justice, entitled *The Challenge of Crime in a Free Society,* the commission suggests:

> From another viewpoint, crime is caused by public tolerance of it, or reluctance or inability to take action against it. Corporate and business--"white collar"--crime is closely associated with a widespread notion that, when making money is involved, anything goes. . . .

In a sense, social and economic conditions "cause" crime. Crime flourishes, and always has flourished, in city slums, those neighborhoods where overcrowding, economic deprivation, social disruption and racial discrimination are endemic. Crime flourishes in conditions of affluence, where there is much desire for material goods and many opportunities to acquire them illegally. Crime flourishes where there are many restless, relatively footloose young people in the population. Crime flourishes when standards of morality are changing rapidly.[42]

Crime, it seems, as a factor of life in Western society, is not a new concept.

Considerable evidence exists that America's large corporations, in adherence with the value system of American business, move to influence legislation, and even legislators, for profit and gain. Constant monitoring by governmental agencies, empowered to enforce particular regulatory codes, is a result of this. Sutherland, in *White Collar Crime* defined white-collar crime as a crime done by a person of high social status within the course of his occupation. He specifically excluded from his definition those crimes such as murder and rape, which were done outside the realm of business dealings.[43] Sutherland suggested that virtually all of the major corporations of America were, in their violation of law, full-time professional criminals.

In a redefinition of the concept, Herbert Ederhertz suggests that white-collar crime is that act or series of acts which are done without resort to physical means and which have to do with concealment or guile for the purposes of obtaining money or property, concealment or guile for the purposes of avoiding payment or loss of money or property, or to get personal advantage through these activities.[44] This definition would include not only the businessman who creates a respectable organization, but also the tax avoider, the welfare cheater, those making fraudulent claims for social security or personal bankruptcy, or those who purchase items with no intention of paying for them.

Inherent in this approach to white-collar crime is the illegal manipulation of a system by someone who has reason to gain by so doing. It also suggests that the white-collar criminal has an understanding of the system and some part of its operation. Our Joe, in order to avoid being caught doing his act, has to understand the internal procedures of a particular part of a bureaucratic or industrial operation, has to speculate as to how he should act in this regard, and has to evaluate his chances for success or failure in the case of exposure. Obviously, he has to have learned how to function within a subsystem of a particular legitimate system of society.

Sociological study of white-collar crime arose with industrialization. At the foremost, as with Sutherland, industry itself

provided the documented evidence that those within it were committing acts opposed to the moral (and especially, the criminal)
code. As American society moved from the Civil War on through
the post-Depression years with the large variety of governmental
agencies--first created for support of a hungry and jobless population and later for the distribution of government stamps and relief
for World War II population--a new type of bureaucracy created
opportunities for a new type of white-collar crime.

In addition to the numerous examples of white-collar crimes
perpetrated by big business and industry and documented by
sociologists, the little guy, too, has taken advantage of system
manipulation in order to profit beyond entitlement.[45] In their book
Criminology: Crime and Criminality, Hasket and Yablonsky wrote
in 1978 that

> the profit system and the principle of caveat emptor have
> widespread support. The leisure class psychology, with its
> emphasis on material wealth and spending, exerts a great
> influence on all strata of our society. Getting something for
> nothing or for as little as possible is acceptable behavior for
> businessmen and workers alike. The businessman may pad his
> expense account, inflate his deductions on his income tax
> return, exaggerate insurance claims, and overcharge when he
> can. The worker may goldbrick on his job, take as many breaks
> as possible, feign illness, and use other methods available to
> him to cheat his employer.[46]

Yet, if we agree with Sutherland that criminal behavior is
learned behavior, learned when the balance of values in favor of
violation of criminal codes is greater than that against, then those
who engage in behavior that seeks to outsmart, to corrupt, to mis-
represent also are products of a learning procedure; this suggests
that such behavior is acceptable to certain segments in our society.
Just how prevalent this type of behavior is to American society is
difficult to determine. Exactly how one businessman allows himself to bribe federal officials and politicians, while another refuses
to do so, is hard to determine. Page Smith, writing about equity
funding (and quoted by Haskell and Yablonsky) concluded: "The
success of American capitalism--indeed its very existence--has
been dependent on the Protestant ethic. That moral code has
always, if sometimes fitfully, imposed restraints, essentially
moral in character, which have prevented capitalism from
devouring us in its lust for power and profits."[47] It is perhaps the
very nature of bureaucratic crime, that is, the type of crime just
described, that it is committed not against one individual but
against a system. This type of crime allows one's moral values to
be less sharply defined than crime against a personal victim,
whether that victim is raped, robbed, or cheated, for it occurs

against a system--a bureaucracy, faceless and impersonal. If one is involved with a bureaucratic crime, if that temptation is against a faceless, impersonal opponent, then does Joe proceed at criminality at a different speed than he would in other situations?

Joseph Bensman and Robert Lilienfield discuss the difficulties engendered when public and corporate officials are faced with choices between public morality and the need to remain a member of an ingroup whose morality may be different from that publicly expressed. They consider how one balances one's need to follow various ethical codes while still other ethics pull behavior into nonacceptable avenues.[48]

In American society, the person who cheats by registering a dog for Medicaid fully recognizes that that action will evoke disapproval by some--not all--segments of a quasiprivate network, but that everyone in that network will know that the action violates both the moral and legal standards of the larger society. Bensman and Lilienfield address these and related issues. Bureaucratic crime allows one to drift constantly between two types of citizenhood, legal and illegal.[49]

Businessmen and corporations have been at the heart of most of the literature about white-collar crime. Less has been written about the deviant acts of professional persons and workers in small-scale occupational settings. Yet employee thefts are responsible for huge losses from industry and consumers. Norman Jaspan, in *The Thief in the White Collar,* notes that bonded losses from employee thefts and other employee dishonesty were difficult to estimate since less than 10 percent of small businesses in the United States are covered by theft insurance. Even more difficult to estimate are the losses resulting from corruption of social agency employees and the recipients of governmental assistance, such as welfare, Medicaid, food stamps, and other public assistance programs.[50]

Most research on embezzlement has focused on the traits of the embezzler and emphasized the violator's personal characteristics. Little has been written on the situational contexts that may contribute to violations of trust. However, a study of public attitudes seems to indicate that if an individual were forced to choose the size of an organization from which he would steal, he would first do so from large businesses, then from governmental agencies, and last from small businesses. It appears that two considerations influenced those who participated. The first was that of detection risk, and the second, the principle of least evil.[51]

Thus, in the United States, it appears that the more removed one is from a personal relationship, the more one is able to shelter one's personal moral system.

Since the largest body of work on immigration and immigrant crime dealt with an immigrant who came into an industrialized society with marginal skills and who had to develop alternative avenues for success, we are left without a body of work to document how well the immigrant who came here skilled in those industrial or social applications needed to enter society as a coequal member fared. Much of the literature about German Jews who came to this country depicts them as able to travel, if not in the establishment, at least in parallel avenues.[52] Presumably their cultural and social status was such that they could continue their pursuits in this country even though they were not a part of the established system.

American sociologists have looked to immigrant crime from a wide variety of perspectives. Various concepts of causation for immigrant crime have been suggested. The "partial failure of the normal mechanisms of social control"[53] as a feature of social disorganization plays a large part in sociological literature. This concept looks to urban slums as instrumental in the weakening of family ties, thereby causing children who have not already "acquired life-organizations based on habits of conventional behavior . . . to become easily subject to the positive influences of . . . the organized rewards of underworld criminal organizations."[54]

Intertwined with this theory in some way is the concept that the American success ethic causes immigrant crime. Unlike the social-disorganization theories, which look to breakdowns of relationships and morale among groups of interrelated persons so as to impair the functions of the society or smaller organization, these theories see immigrants as being unable to achieve success in terms of power and economic rewards through legitimate means and, therefore, being impelled to choose criminal or illegitimate means to do so. This theory holds that many immigrants use any means available to rise through the ranks of American systems, understanding upon immigration what they are and what the very essence of the American success ethic is.

Another proposed sociological answer to immigrant crime, to repeat, is Sutherland's. His theory of differential association suggests that the immigrant, housed in urban slum areas, learns criminality after arriving on these shores, through contact or association with groups having values favorable toward criminality. This theory of criminality, although seminal in the thinking of sociologists, leaves open the question of why people choose the associations they do, how immigrants discover the crimes appropriate to their new society, and how those who arrived as adults negate noncriminal conditioning (if indeed there was such) in their early years in their native country. Sutherland's theory seems to suggest, at least in part, that the immigrant has arrived on these shores as a sort of tabula rasa, upon which the grime of urban criminal patterns leaves the first mark.

Additionally, immigrants have for the most part been regarded as a totality, a picture evoked by Ellis Island photographs. They are seen as a shadowy whole, dressed in foreign attire, high-top shoes, babushkas on their heads, or their hands stained dark from years of potato digging in the field, hardly comforting to behold. Indeed, they were an embarrassment to those who had come before them, even those from the same lands. The new immigrants, those studied by sociologists, were a fascinating if uncomfortable group upon which to base theory. It was their ghettos, their slums, their crimes and their attempts to elevate their status that provided the basis of so much of the literature on crime and criminal behavior that we read today.[55]

Indeed, the immigrations of the late 19th and early 20th centuries did change the very character of the land. But in dealing with the criminality in these immigrations, it seems that one must examine the various case histories of the immigrants in order to look at their criminality. There are several possibilities at which one must look. Did our Joe, from an agrarian, underdeveloped nation, arrive in modern society with little background contingency on which to base his expectancies? Or when he arrived here did he carry with him some quasicriminal attitudes and backgrounds applicable to our own society? Joe, in his home society might or might not have had criminal patterns and opportunities, might or might not have associated with elements that violated the code of a society where there seems to be little personal deviation.[56]

Conversely, Joe could have come from an urban society where he might or might not have engaged in criminal behavior, and his criminal behavior might have been of many varieties. He might have been part of a small social subsystem that engaged in overtly illegal behavior, such as robbery and violent crimes, or he might have been more subtle in his criminality, understanding the nature of his social order and acting with it in an adverse but personally profitable manner.

If Joe came from a society approximating our society, then one must ask whether, upon immigration or within a short time thereafter, he can directly translate to his new environment the criminal behaviors he carried out in his native country. What qualities are necessary for this kind of direct transformation, if indeed there are such? Does he have to act criminally only with those who immigrated with him, or can he extend his behavior beyond that, and what are the factors necessary to do so? Does he learn the American success ethic upon immigration or did he come with an already in-place ethic of success similar to that found in the literature about American crime?

Of interest then is just how a group brings with it its cultural learnings and how able it is to impose these cultural learnings on American society, which sees success as a major goal. If one enters a country with similar patterns to those of one's country of origin, can one do so without resort to criminality? Or, if one has developed criminal patterns in the home country, can one impose them upon immigration to a country that cannot adopt them (surely classical banditry would not have a place in criminal networks here). What happens when the crime of country A can be directly translated to the crime of country B, the new home?

Since 1965, as a result of changes in the U. S. Immigration Law, a new type of immigrant has arrived on the American scene. This immigrant is one who comes from an urban technological society, has had schooling in the working of modern industrial materials and theories, has skills that in many instances are directly translatable to the American economy, which often has an open acceptance of them, and are either middle class or blue collar in orientation. This new, post-1965 immigrant, like those from the Soviet Union, represents another society--which in some ways directly parallels and in other ways is merely similar to ours--and is rather a unique immigrant to study. It is perhaps of value then to look at these immigrants in their home country and then in their new country and to examine how they transform their cultural values and, in some instances, their criminal values into the culture of our society. Does their cultural template prepare them for a direct transformation?

Since many of these new Russian immigrants have settled in the metropolitan area, with a particularly large number making their home in the Brighton Beach section of Brooklyn, we have at hand the means of examining some of the criminal systems functioning in the Soviet Union and then determining whether, how, and by whom they are applied here. This new immigration, referred to in the Soviet immigrant community as the third immigration of Russians to these shores, differs from the first two in that, for the first time, it consists of people who have spent their whole lives under the Soviet communist system. Whereas the first immigration came before the institution of the socialist state, and the second shortly thereafter, this one provides us with a population that has lived its whole life under a social order claiming to provide all its citizens with all the economic goods and material possessions necessary for life. In effect, this immigration comes to us from a nation with a governmental bureaucracy unparalleled in size even by that in our own country. It is not an immigration of "the tired, the poor, the huddled [peasant] masses yearning to be free"; rather, it is largely skilled, of urban origins, and middle class, by American socioeconomic standards, in its desires and aspirations.

This new immigration and its particular immigrant can provide us with some reexamination of the theoretical perspectives on immigrant crime and criminal patterns.

NOTES

1 Emile Durkheim, The Division of Labor in Society, trans. G. Simpson (New York: The Free Press, 1965).

2 Ibid.

3 Emile Durkheim, The Rules of the Sociological Method, trans. Sarah A. Solovay and John H. Mueller; George E. G. Catlin, ed. (New York: The Free Press, 1965).

4 Robert Merton, "Social Structure and Anomie," American Sociological Review 3, No. 5 (October 1938), p. 672.

5 Ibid.

6 Ibid., p. 680.

7 For a discussion of the concept of Anglicizing a population see Anthony Platt "The Triumph of Benevolence: The Origins of the Juvenile Justice System in the United States" in Criminal Justice in America, Richard Quinney, ed. (Bsoton: Little Brown, 1974), pp. 366-384.

8 Irving Howe, World of Our Fathers (New York: Harcourt, Brace and Jovanovich, 1976), p. 263.

9 Ibid.

10 Viola Klein, Feminine Character: History of an Idealogy (Urbana: Univ. of Illinois Press, 1973), pp. 16-19.

11 Quoted in Edith Elmer Wood, The Housing of the Unskilled Wage Earner (New York: Macmillian, 1919), p. 29.

12 Marshall B. Clinard and Daniel J. Abbott, Crime In Developing Countries, A Comparative Perspective (New York: Wiley, 1973).

13 George Herbert Mead, in Mind, Self and Society, Charles W. Merris, ed. (Chicago: Univ. of Chicago Press, 1970), calls this "the self as a social construct." Charles H. Cooley, in Social Organization (New York Scribner, 1909), calls this "the looking glass self." Albert Cohen, in Deviance and Control (Englewood Cliffs, N.J.: Prentice Hall, 1966), describes it as "the self . . . built up in the process of interacting with others."

14   Marshall B. Clinard and Robert F. Meier, Sociology of Deviant Behavior (New York: Holt, Rinehart and Winston, 1979).

15   Elliot Lebow, Tally's Corner (Boston: Little, Brown and Co. 1967).

16   Irving Pillavin and Carl Werthman, "Gang Members and Ecological Conflict," Rose Giallombardo, ed., Juvenile Delinquency 3rd ed. (New York: John Wiley and Sons, Inc.) pp. 305-325.

17   Edwin H. Sutherland and Donald R. Cressey, Criminology, 8th ed., (Philadphia: J.B. Lippincott Co. 1970), p. 75.

18   Edwin H. Sutherland and Donald R. Cressey, "Theory of Differential Association," Criminology 9th ed. (Philadelphia: J.B. Lippincott Co. 1974), p. 76.

19   Ibid., p. 77.

20   W. I. Thomas and Florian Znaniecki, Polish Peasant in Europe and America (New York: Alfred A. Knopf, 1918).

21   Clifford Shaw, Delinquency Areas (Chicago: University of Chicago Press, 1929).

22   Sutherland, Principals of Criminology, 1939 ed.

23   Donald R. Cressey, "The Theory of Differential Association: An Introduction." Social Problems, 8 (Summer 1960), pp. 2-68.

24   Sutherland, Principals of Criminology, 9th ed.

25   Robert E. Park, "Human Migration and the Marginal Man," Race and Culture (Glencoe, Ill: The Free Press, 1950), pp. 345-356.

26   For a discussion of these theories see Clifford R. Shaw and Henry D. McKay, Juvenile Delinquency and Urban Areas (Chicago: University of Chicago Press 1942).

27   Gunnar Myrdal, An American Dilemma (New York: Harper & Row, 1944).

28   Charles Horton Cooley, Human Nature and the Social Order (New York: Schocken, 1964).

[29] C. Wright Mills, The Sociological Imagination (New York: Oxford University Press, 1959), pp. 131-154.

[30] Daniel Bell, "Crime as an American Way of Life," Antioch Review, 13 (June 1953), pp. 131-154.

[31] Edmund Cahn, The Moral Decision, (Bloomington: Indiana University Press, 1956).

[32] Bell, p. 132.

[33] Milton L. Barron "The Criminogenic Society: Social Values and Deviance," Current Perspectives on Criminal Behavior, ed. Abraham S. Blumberg (New York: Alfred A. Knopf, 1974), pp. 68-86.

[34] Bell, p. 133.

[35] Francis A. J. Ianni, Black Mafia (New York: Simon and Schuster, 1974).

[36] Charles Silberman, Criminal Justice, Criminal Violence (New York: Random House, 1978), p. 36.

[37] Ibid. p. 37.

[38] Ibid.

[39] Daniel Bell, "The Last of the Business Rackets," Fortune, June 1951.

[40] See Donald Cressey, Theft of the Nation (New York: Harper & Row, 1969) and Francis A. J. Ianni, ed. Francis A. J. Ianni and Elizabeth Reuss Ianni, The Crime Society: Organized Crime and Corruption in America (New American Library, 1976).

[41] Tony McAdams and Robert C. Miljus, "Growing Criminal Liability of Executives," Harvard Business Review 55 (1977), pp. 36-39.

[42] President's Commission on Law Enforcement and Administration of Justice, The Challenge of Crime in a Free Society (U.S. Government Printing Office, 1967).

[43] Sutherland, White Collar Crime, p. 17.

[44] Herbert Edelhertz, Nature, Impact, Prosecution of White Collar Crime (Washington, D.C., U.S. Govt. Printing Office, 1970) p. 12.

[45] See Philip M. Stern, "Uncle Sam's Welfare Program - for the Rich," New York Times Magazine, April 16, 1972, p. 26, Ralph Nader and Kate Blackwell, You and Your Pension (New York: Grossman Publishers, 1973), Edward A. Ross, "The Criminaloid," in White Collar Criminal, ed. Gilbert Geis (New York: Atherton, 1968) for a discussion of these issues.

[46] Martin R. Haskell and Lewis Yablonsky, Criminology: Crime and Criminality 2nd ed. (Chicago: Rand McNally College Publishing, 1978), p. 199.

[47] Haskel and Yablonsky, p. 202.

[48] Joseph Bensman and Robert Lilienfeld, Between Public and Private: Lost Boundaries of the Self (New York: The Free Press, 1979).

[49] For a full discussion of drift see David Matza, Delinquency and Drift (New York: Wiley, 1966).

[50] Norman Jaspan, The Thief in the White Collar (Philadelphia: J. B. Lippincott 1960), p. 234.

[51] Erwin O. Smigel "Public Attitude Toward Stealing as Related to the Size of the Victim Organization," American Sociological Review, 21 (June 1956) pp. 320-327.

[52] See Stephen Birmingham, Our Crowd (New York: Harper and Row 1967) for a detailed depiction of the entry of the German Jews into America's monied communities.

[53] See Robert E. L. Faris, Social Disorganization 2nd ed. (New York: Ronald Press, 1955) for discussion of the concept of weakening family ties in the ghetto.

[54] Faris, p. 246.

[55] See Max I. Dimont, The Jews in America (New York: Simon and Shuster, 1978), Daniel J. Boorstin, The Americans: The Colonial Experience (New York: Vintage Books, 1958), Allan Nevins and H. Steele Commager, A Pocket History of the United States (New York: Pocket Books, 1967).

[56] See Robert Redfield, "The Folk Society," American Journal of Sociology 52, (January 1947).

CHAPTER 4

An Ethnographic Study: Brighton Beach

This study was undertaken to assess the effects of coming from a system that favors criminality into one where criminal values are less salient. Although there is a Russian immigration to many cities in the United States, this study was limited to the New York area, which houses the largest portion of this immigration.[1] In addition, this is a qualitative study because the new Russian immigrants distrust written questionnaires, having had only bad experiences with bureaucratic forms and work papers. Equally, they distrust people who they perceive as representatives of official agencies. These new arrivals tend to view all such social agencies or research personnel as an arm of the government because they have had no experience either with private charity or private universities in their homeland.[2]

The concept of nongovernmental research does not exist in the USSR: research is only conducted for the government and by the government. Because of this and because in their home country it was unwise to give out information to strangers, this immigrant population functions with understandings about strangers, questions, and academic research that differ markedly from those of the population brought up in the United States. In addition, as discussed in Chapter 3, members of this population are skillful at deceit. Having been brought up with a defensive attitude toward strangers and questioners, the Russians--like certain American populations, for example, the mountain folks who looked upon strangers as revenue men during prohibition--respond to any questions with caution. Because of this, interviews conducted by

Americans with new Russians are often inaccurate. The Russian population has learned through intensive cultural training, derived through a lifetime of practice in the USSR, how to provide desired answers--that is the answers that they feel the questioner wants to hear or those that will protect the respondent from official hazing. This cultural training makes it particularly difficult to examine the feelings of this new population.

These difficulties in formal interviewing were considered in planning this study. Therefore, information was collected in several ways. Preliminary observations conducted by myself over the past ten years were subjected to systematic recollection and analysis. I have observed the immigration and resettlement of new Russian immigrants because of my interest in their problems and because of my fluency in their language. Therefore, I have been the recipient of many confidences and of much personal information. In addition, I have visited the Soviet Union in the company of another fluent Russian-speaking person. While there I was able to interview many Russians in private situations where they did not feel the constraints of governmental censorship. As an observer, I was able to ascertain which areas of their lives were most like those in the United States and which were the most different.

American literature on criminality in the USSR is largely limited to the observations of the few Americans who were allowed some access to the Russian scene and to the observations of the few recent immigrants who are able to describe their own previous personal experiences. The official literature emanating from the USSR is clouded with misinformation. Konstantin Simis has discussed corruption in the Soviet Army and describes how party officials work to squelch recognition of this. He comments on the fact that recently, and for the first time, articles on corruption in the Red Army have begun to appear.

> All Soviet newspapers adhere to a strict ban on publishing information about corruption in the Communist Party apparatus, the KGB and the top brass. This taboo could only be broken by permission from higher up, permission given thanks to the campaign to expose corruption initiated by Yuri Andropov immediately after he came to power.
> For many years Soviet propaganda media have created an idealized image [of the military].[3]

Simis comments with surprise on how the Soviets have even now allowed such information to reach the press. He too functions with the understandings that pervade the Soviet citizen's concept of government. That is, that everything is clouded with deceit.

Thus, information on criminality in the Soviet system was gained through a limited literature and through informants who told of their personal experiences while dealing with life in the USSR. The informants were all people who had not achieved high rank within the party apparatus and who therefore were limited in the totality of their own observations. For this study I specifically interviewed 35 new Russian immigrants. My interviews were conducted in Russian. The new immigrants were assured that no material discussed with me would be attributed to them by name, and that my interest in the subject about which they were questioned was academic in nature. Because of my fluency with the language and my already developed familiarity with immigrant community life, the respondents were cooperative and often referred me to others in their community who they felt would also be helpful, thus creating in effect a snowball sample. These Russians were interested in my language proficiency. I felt I was able to gain their trust by explaining that my parents had come over under similar circumstances as they, and I had become an American in one generation.

The members of this community were careful to explain to me that they were well aware of the large amount of criminal activity carried on by the new Russians. They would not discuss this in public places, but only in private or in the privacy of their homes. They expressed opinions about the fact that their immigration included many "bad people," as they term it.

This term, "bad people," or *plokhiye lyudi*, seems to use the word "bad" in the same fashion as a mother would in describing another child with whom she does not want her child to play. "That child is bad," she might say. "I don't want you near him." The *plokhiye lyudi* are looked upon in effect as unfit companions for "good people." They are viewed as an outlaw population whose influence one must consciously avoid so as not to become bad as well.

Although at first many were unwilling to describe specific areas of criminality (that is, they would only describe those about which I already had expressed knowledge), as I became more and more versed in the machinations within their community they consented to describe these activities in detail. Information I gained from American sources who know this new Russian immigration was therefore useful not only in adding to my knowledge of the criminal patterns of this Russian immigration but also in validating the information of the Russian informants and in encouraring them to talk about ever-widening criminal experiences. In effect, their hints about bad people were explained to me by Americans who knew from first-hand experience exactly what kind of bad people these new Russians meant. This will be explained more fully as this chapter unfolds.

Many denied that their own particular family was heavily involved in theft or bribery, but all agreed that the people around them had illegal dealings of one sort or another. These dealings include many activities, moving up a scale from cash transactions that avoid tax liability to false documents being presented to governmental agencies to major criminal activities. These are documented further in this chapter under specific criminal categories.

There was a general agreement among these new immigrants that those who were involved with what they termed "loftier" thoughts--that is, dissidents and intellectuals--did not get as heavily involved in illegal economic activity either in the USSR or here. However, they agreed that these people made do without caring for the amenities of daily life, clothes and good food, for which craftiness and illegality were necessary. They had, of course, to be careful about political surveillance and entrapment, since much of their behavior was considered to be politically illegal.

In addition to my interviews with new Russian immigrants, I conducted interviews with Americans who are especially familiar with them. These included several people involved in their resettlement (both on an official and an unofficial basis) and members of the Brighton Beach community who work and/or live with them. Several community leaders, workers in community facilities that help the population, and professional New York detectives and patrolmen were also interviewed, as were federal law-enforcement personnel.[4] Also interviewed were several new Russian immigrants who are not members of the Brighton Beach community and who work in professions or intellectual pursuits that, both in their homeland and in the United States, set them apart from the major study population.

Primarily, then, the population studied is based in New York City and has chosen to reside in Brighton Beach, Brooklyn. Many of the residents of the community are from Odessa, which, like Brighton, is situated on the shores of a large body of water. Although this may appear as a process of self-selection and thus not typical of all Russians, this population has been augmented by others who come from other parts of the Soviet Union.

The Brighton Beach area houses approximately 30,000 new Russian immigrants out of a total population of 75,000 and is the largest Russian community in the United States. It is primarily a neighborhood of blue-collar workers and small business owners. Most of its residents were not involved in professional or intellectual activities in the USSR. The majority who moved to Brighton Beach were, while in the USSR, employed on nonprofessional or "specialty" activities. Generally they had direct dealings in goods, and thus had trades that allowed them to have, by Soviet definition, a specialty: a shoemaker has a specialty, whereas an engineer does not. One handles the product of the specialty directly and therefore can trade with it. A shoemaker has extra shoes with which to trade. He is in possession of a commodity with value on the open market. He controls something that allows him extra barter ability. In the Soviet Union this ability (as explained in Chap. 2) allows for a higher standard of living.

This study concerns itself both with people who had and did not have specialties but not with people who were professionals. Those who had professions were at a disadvantage in the USSR because it was difficult for them to gain access to the goods that allowed them extra barter opportunities and thus more income. For example, one man had run a government car pool and was in charge of distributing cars to governmental employees when they needed them. He had the power to decide which people got which cars and in what time period, and of course, he could make his decisions in favor of those who could supply him with the various end products of their businesses. If the foreman of a manufacturing plant brought in a coat, that foreman would be sure to get a car ahead of another person who could not provide such a useful item. If an inspector of meat plants needed a car for a visit to the plants, the man who ran the car pool could demand meat in return for his dispensation of a scarce car to the inspector. So although this man did not have a specialty, he nevertheless was able to deal in barterable services.

Professionals had few such opportunities. Unless they were able to travel and acquire goods either outside the USSR or in other parts of it, they were limited to making do on their government salary. Physicians, however, got "gifts" for special or immediate treatment. Teachers got gifts from parents to look after their children. Thus, the population studied is the one which, while in the USSR, had the most contact with goods and services and which became adept in the manipulation of the system. Additionally, there is a population of senior citizens, parents of younger emigres who--although they do not work here in the United States--participate in a variety of social programs for which they are eligible because of their age. This older population is of interest to us because of their eligibility for social benefits and their ability to manipulate our system. They are however, only tangentially included in this study.

Through interviews with new Russian immigrants and with others familiar with this group, certain understandings emerge. There are assumptions that are partly taken for granted and are rarely mentioned explicitly, which nonetheless underly the immigrants' behavior. They emerge through facial gestures, shrugs, and furrowed brows. Some of these understandings are only visible to those who know the Russian's proclivity for withdrawal when approached by an authority figure or a stranger. The smile and the polite response appear to contain nothing of a devious nature. Yet this population has to function on the understandings that provided the means of survival in their home country. They had to determine quickly who could do harm and who could not. They had to make an on-the-spot decision about how to respond. It is difficult for most Americans to understand much of this kind of behavior, which is part of daily Soviet life. Perhaps a black person from New York, driving through the South during the freedom marches, could understand. But this new Russian population has not only the type of understanding just illustrated, but it also brings from its experiences in another land a wide variety of understandings which it applies and misapplies to situations and experiences in this, their new land.

These understandings are, first, about the new immigrant group in particular and about their transference or cultural learnings from the USSR; and, second, about members of the group individually and their transference of skills and abilities in order to operate in a new system. I have organized these understandings into two basic charts. Chart 1 compares the cultural understandings of the total population as they apply to criminologic values in the USSR and in the United States; Chart 2 deals with three categories of new Russian immigrants and compares their activities in the USSR and how they apply them in the United States. Each chart has been cross-checked with people familiar with the new Russian community and with people in it. All agree that the incoming Russians, even those without criminologic patterns, surpass their American counterparts in their skill of manipulation and understanding of the hidden dimensions of speech and actions.

The left side of Chart 1 shows the ramifications of the Russians' common understanding that every party apparat--upper-level, mid-level, and lower-level--is involved in massive corruption. Proof of this is visible to all Soviet citizens at their place of work, point of purchase for foodstuffs, and in the very apartment buildings in which they live. This common understanding that the establishment is crooked and that laws are enforced erratically and in a discretionary fashion persuades the population that the only way to succeed is through circumvention of official procedures and laws. As detailed in Chapter 2, allies are needed for successful circumvention of public procedures. Power also lies in the ability to control goods and services, to manipulate paper, and to trade off favors for favors.

The trading of favors creates a situation in which all Russians are potentially guilty of violation of the law. For example, the car-pool manager has taken goods, that is, a coat for himself or someone in his family. Therefore, he is guilty of a crime against the government. The person who gave him the coat is also guilty, since he has stolen government property. The meat inspector knows that he should not dispense meat as in a private enterprise. He is guilty, and so is the man who gave the bribe. Each has the other over the proverbial barrel. This method of enforcement--*Shantazh*, which means "blackmailing"--is used throughout the Soviet system to affirm cooperation and loyalty to those who operate within one's sphere. *Shantazh* has traveled from the USSR to the United States with the new Russian immigrants.

These criminologic understandings in the USSR are described and illustrated in Chapter 2. The criminologic understandings of new Russian immigrants in the United States are discussed in this chapter. The Chart, compiled from interviews, summarizes the understandings of the new Russian immigrants. It must be pointed out that the summary of criminologic understandings in the United States reflects not only the population involved in actual criminal activities but rather the total new Russian immigrant population's understandings, whether or not they themselves are involved in criminal activities here in the United States.

Chart 1

Criminologic Understandings of the

"New" Russian Immigrants

There	*Here*
1. Establishment is crooked.	1. Establishment is lax.
2. Fear of law and enforcers is constant.	2. Fear of law and enforcers is minimal.
3. Jurisdictional division of authority is understood.	3. Jurisdictional division of federal, state, and agency authority is not understood.
4. Agents of law enforcement are arbitrary and erratic.	4. Agents of law enforcement are naive or stupid.
5. Circumvention is the only way to succeed; one must learn paper and travel circumvention.	5. Circumvention is easy and often unnecessary for success; one needs little paper and travel circum-vention.

Chart 2

Kinds of Criminals: The USSR and the United States

	There	*Here*
	necessary criminal	system beater
Survivor		
	criminal	system beater*
Connivor	criminal	criminal

*Includes violations of law in dealing with bureaucratic agencies.

NOTES

[1] National Conference on Soviet Jewry: Jewish Emigration from the USSR Statistics.

[2] See Betty Brodsky, "Natural Support Systems for Mental Health Problems and the Soviet Jewish Emigre Community," working paper.

[3] Simis, "Corrupt Army," Miami Herald 29 January 1984. Also see The "Liberators": My Life in the Soviet Army, Viktor Suvorov (New York: W. W. Norton 1983).

[4] Because much of the information about the new Russian immigrants is still of a confidential nature and circulated only between police departments of various major American, Canadian, European and Israeli law enforcement agencies, it is impossible to cite sources who were considerate and cooperative enough to share such information with me. When possible throughout the rest of the citations, I will attempt to identify the city or agency which allowed me to share in its confidential interagency material.

CHAPTER 5

Immigrant Assumptions about Crime and Law

ESTABLISHMENT IS LAX

Once the new Russians have immigrated, they search for familiar patterns of life in their new country. Since childhood, they have been interpreting experiences and situations through learnings about their society. These have provided the only way of gauging experience. Therefore, immigrants must resort to previously held understandings to interpret the new situations they confront in their new land. Both the new Russians who continue to engage in criminality and those who, as will be explained in Chart 2 (Ch. 4), rely on familiar old-country systems for survival here, gauge our system of law and our law-enforcement agents against a pattern developed throughout their life in their home country. They look to see how the law-enforcement agencies treat those who they know are doing "bad" things here. Their discovery of minimal enforcement activities around them, or what they perceive as minimal enforcement activities, persuades them that U.S. law-enforcement agencies and their agents are weak and naive. "The FBI actually called me three times for an appointment," said G.S. with a laugh. Her comments were balanced by knowledge that had agents of the KGB wanted to speak to her in the USSR, there would be no phone call, no attempt to make an appointment. Similarly, G.S. felt that the manner in which the FBI asked questions was not in keeping with their reputation as a major American law-enforcement agency. "They were respectful and polite," she said. Her manner indicated that this type of behavior belied their position as agents of a branch of government. Having learned from the KGB just how such agents were "supposed" to act, even while fearing them and cursing them, she nevertheless can judge behavior of law-enforcement personnel only by reference to their example. Therefore, G.S. reasons that if the agents are unthreatening and polite, they cannot be doing a good job.

M.S. states that criminals in the United States are allowed to walk around on the streets. The concept of due process is so alien to the understandings of the new Russians that no amount of explanation is satisfactory. M.G. asked, "But why, if you think that someone stole or robbed or raped someone, do you let them out?" No matter how hard I have tried to explain to her that suspicion of a crime is not enough evidence to keep a person in jail, she responds: "But that is why your streets are filled with criminals." M.S. and G.S., both of whom are women under forty and in this country for less than five years, are fearful for their personal safety in a way they were never fearful before. To them, due process only means that our police are weak and our system does not scare people enough.

FEAR OF LAW ENFORCEMENT IS MINIMAL

Since the prevailing emotion of fear governed their lives in the USSR, they see the very lack of fear as evidence that the American law-enforcement system permits an atmosphere in which thieves thrive and criminals are encouraged to continue their acts. L.R. asserts that in summer, the nearby area of Brighton Beach is a haven for junkies from other areas of Brooklyn and from the metropolitan area. She comments that even though there is a police presence during the summer months, the police do not seem to do anything to stop the criminal element from coming into her neighborhood. "There is a subway stop here and in the summer they come right down the steps and go to the beach. The place is disgusting and people are doing bad things. It is so obvious and yet the police do not do very much about it at all. No one even cares if the police are around, they just go on doing it." Within the community itself there is a feeling that the law-enforcement authorities are impotent when it comes to stopping the continuous and numerous thefts and burglaries in Brighton Beach. S.R., a recent immigrant and a resident of one of the side streets near Coney Island Avenue, describes the amount of crime in her area: "Most of the stores have been robbed and there is nothing anyone has done. Maybe it is because people know who did it and do not tell because they are more afraid of the thieves than they are of the police." J.S., a local community leader whose agency deals with the new Russian population, has had discussions with many new Russians about the crime in the area. He says that those who do not commit criminal acts of major proportion themselves, view the vast amount of crime as evidence of the ineffectiveness of the American law-enforcement agencies. Thus, in dealing with American crime on the street, the immigrants identify with the stringent law-enforcement and arbitrariness of the Soviet system.

MISUNDERSTANDING OF JURISDICTION

The new Russians find it difficult to understand the legal juris-diction of governmental law-enforcement agencies. It is hard for someone who knows only one supreme legal power (and that vested in the Soviet government) to understand that there are various agencies, most of which have jurisdictional control over particular acts.

The concept of states' rights or of limited powers, as it exists in the United States, is baffling for many immigrants. They are used to the supremacy of the state and it is therefore difficult for them to understand America's division of powers. For example, a nightclub that dispenses liquor without a license will be investi-gated by the state liquor authority, the police, and possibly an arm of the Internal Revenue Service, but each investigation will be a separate one.

J.C., a member of the New York City Police Department's Intelligence Division, describes an incident that is merely humorous to Americans, but which--to a new immigrant unfamiliar with the laws of the land--is an operation explained by the understanding available to him from his prior culture. J.C. describes a man who was involved in illegal activities while in Canada, whose car was seized by the Royal Canadian Mounted Police:

> He comes back here to New York and he reports that his car was stolen while he was in Canada. The New York police launch an investigation and they get in touch with the Canadian authorities in Toronto. They come back with the information that his car was seized and not only that--that he signed an understanding that it was seized. Still, he thought that he could report the car stolen and get away with it. He just had no idea that he could be found out.

In addition, modern technology has made interagency cooperation even easier. J.C. suggests that without such technology many offenders would, and often still do, fall through the cracks. "Just a few years ago we would not be able to catch up with many of these people. But computers have made interagency cooperation a lot easier."

P.G., a detective of the Joint Organized Crime Task Force, an interagency team uniting the various jurisdictions dealing with organized crime, describes the way the Russians move throughout the country: "A lot of them do things interstate. Then their stolen property winds up as cash. But even if there is a federal warrant, a fugitive warrant, they pull this thing and then come back to Brighton. Then they do things in Brighton and think they can't be found." A major police report describes the many cities tied together through the investigation of one criminal of new Russian extraction:

> [A] spectacular crime reported was the October 10, 1981, robbery of a Russian woman of $50,000 in cash that the woman, who was visiting from Vienna, Austria, was going to use to buy a condominium in Philadelphia. The woman was taken to New York to pick up the $50,000 at a bank, but was delayed in New York, so she could not arrive in Philadelphia in time to deposit the money in a bank. The person who both drove her to New York and delayed her is a 35-year-old associate of [a] welfare recipient, who is the owner of an antique store in New York, and is in the process of purchasing what is believed to be the meeting place of this Russian criminal organization--a restaurant in Philadelphia. The estimated cost of this restaurant is in excess of $150,000.[1]

It appears that after the delay in New York, the driver pulled into the parking lot of his apartment house and was set upon by three Russian males with guns, who took the cash and fled in an auto, later reported stolen from a Soviet immigrant from Brighton. During the investigation, numerous discrepancies in the stories of both the alleged victim and the driver were noted. Both were asked to take polygraph tests. The driver submitted and failed, and the complainant refused to be tested. It was determined that the driver of the auto had been arrested previously, once for fraud on a Philadelphia bank and twice for robbery in New York City while he was a cab driver. Additionally, he is currently being investigated by the Pittsburgh district attorney's office for a fraudulent sale of antiques to a Cleveland dealer in 1979. The driver had an antique business in Cleveland in 1976, and, interestingly, was in or near that city when a .38 caliber revolver was reported stolen, a revolver that eventually turned up in the shooting incident in Philadelphia.

The interjurisdictional nature of the activities of some of the more criminally involved new immigrants shows how difficult it was to chart and gather statistics on this population. Since their major criminal activities occur outside of their home district, and since the population is singled out as "immigrant" only until they attain citizenship, documentation is difficult.

POLICE: NAIVE OR STUPID

The 1983 police report states that the new Russian immigrants "find the police soft and easily tricked by the laws which guarantee certain freedoms to accused persons."[2] The new Russian immigrant, viewing the American justice system through a totalitarian schemata, considers it nonthreatening and inefficient. There is little understanding of the concept of due process and even less understanding of the American belief in constitutional guarantees. "Guilty unless proven innocent" is for the new Russian immigrant a much more understandable concept than the American creed, which reverses that statement. "They know that they can get away with it," said M.S. G.P., a little woman from Leningrad who has been in this country for only three years and has to listen to the Yiddish radio station in order to get news, finds it difficult to understand why there is so much crime. "But you are not locking up all the people who do these things. Why are they allowed to walk around the streets before they are locked up?" Attempts to explain the American concepts of guilt and innocence, of bail as a right until guilt is proven, were met with noncomprehension: "But if you know that they did it--if they were caught--why not just lock them up?"

Maya Litvinov, quoted in a *New York Times* article, describes how difficult it is to understand this system of justice:

> We are all children of our own lands. We tend to bring totalitarian solutions to democratic problems and yet we realize that their solutions caused our dissension with the Soviet system. . . . We understand the system of "innocent until proven guilty" because we've worked so long in the area of human rights, but for most immigrants it is a hard concept to grasp, American justice is hard for us to comprehend.[3]

MANIPULABLE BUREAUCRACY

They also see our bureaucratic agencies, human services, housing authorities, and so on as easily manipulated and deceived. The relative harshness of the Russian system, which they have successfully evaded, is used as a standard to disparage the apparently more lenient, disorganized, and jurisdictionally divided system in the United States. Many profit from these bureaucratic failures.

G.R., who has been in this country for five years and lives in the Brighton Beach area, describes the fact that many of those who have businesses in the area are also receiving government assistance: "They put the business in the name of someone who is working, and they collect welfare also. And they live in apartments with eight also." (She is referring to certain rent subsidies provided by the State of New York and popularly referred to as "Section 8.")

Police reports dealing with Russians who are picked up for various offenses seem to validate G.R.'s comments that these people also receive welfare or other governmental assistance. Statements such as "Male described as welfare recipient. . ." and "During the course of the welfare recipient's interview with police. . ." pepper police reports dealing with underworld activity of the new Russian immigrants.[4] But even those who are not involved in major criminality have had enough experience with bureaucratic entitlement to find an easy mark in the American agencies that distribute welfare and other aid.

Among the Americans who deal with the Russian community, many report that that part of the population which comes to the attention of either community agencies or law-enforcement authorities tends to be aggressive, distrustful, and less than truthful when dealing with an authoritarian situation and governmental or bureaucratic personnel. The tendency to use the easy fib, described in Chapter 3, does not leave one's personality upon immigration.

A community worker who works for a not-for-profit agency in the Brighton area states that this population is survival oriented, and suggests that this is a facet of all immigrant groups:

> So they push on line. Maybe that is the worst thing you can say about some of them. And that is said by people in the community who dislike seeing them use governmental funds to which they made no contribution. They do tend to be aggressive and assertive. But the line between aggressive and violations of law is hard to define. They do tend to be demanding. But we try to teach them to negotiate rather than manipulate. They distrusted money and used other means to get their way. Manipulation, gifts and such. They came here demanding jobs, furniture, etc., but they have a sense of public entitlement.

Another American who is involved in community work with the Russians suggests that their method of manipulation rests on the cultural understandings prevalent in their home country: "There is a decrease in manipulation. There was an initial proliferation of gifts to workers. There seems to be a cultural use of gifts, but after a while they realized it was doing more harm than good." This suggests that the Russians are slowly being socialized to American standards.

A worker in a resettlement agency who had been actively involved with the new Russian immigrants described her experience:

People came to me with gifts and I refused them. But I know that they came from Vienna already armed with the names of those who would take "gifts" for services and who would place them in better apartments or such. It was hard to explain to these new Russians that we were not an arm of the government but a private resettlement agency. But I have heard of how they tried to bribe and ingratiate themselves in order to obtain the same rewards they thought they could get there. It is hard for them to understand our system. And I do know of Americans who did accept the gifts, too.

Another major unpublished police report states that the new Russian criminal uses these same skills for furtherance of criminal activities. "The Russian criminal in the Soviet Union spends most of his time paying-off and dodging police officials. [An informant] said Russian criminals living in this country find the police soft and easily tricked because of the laws."[5] It must be conceded that the scope and depth of vision of law-enforcement officials is limited, since many community members go about their business only within the confines of their immediate area and have no contacts with any authorities after they become acclimated to life this country.

"PAPERS" AS IDENTITY

It is difficult for the new immigrants to understand that Americans do not need personal identification papers. Discussions with them of the way Americans can move throughout this country without permission provides an early understanding of the fact that we do not need papers for most of our activities. M.D. describes how different this is from the USSR: "When I wanted to go somewhere else I had to get permission. I could not just go to the airport and get a ticket. And I carried papers to identify me. Mine said I was a Jew."

S.D., a Russian who came to this country on a visit and was then granted asylum, tells how he was able to have an easier life in the USSR: "My papers said I was Polish. When I was in the Army someone changed my papers so they did not say, under nationality, 'Jew.' That made it easier."

L.B., a Russian woman who has been in this country for several years, describes why people could not move into the city even though life in the countryside was harsh: "They had no papers to stay in Moscow. There was no permission for them to live in an apartment in Moscow. They came on the train with the fruits they wanted to sell but then they had to take the train back even if the trip was long."

Russians are convinced of the importance of papers. All their life in the USSR, they had to make sure that they had the right paper, the approved paper, or the revised paper. Therefore, even among those who do not engage in major criminal acts, there are certain understandings regarding the use of paper. Russians who immigrate have to have proper papers for immigration. They must also have proper papers in order to enter this country. Because they find it hard to understand the concept of limited governmental powers and the separation of these powers between state and federal authorities, and because they have had a socialization from childhood stressing the importance of papers, these new immigrants come equipped with old-country understandings surrounding paper and paper manipulation.

M.S., a recent Russian immigrant, describes how she was advised to fraudulently upgrade her academic credentials and thus her job qualifications.

> But you have to understand that when people come here and they do not have the language, they have to find some way to overcome the problems. Many will change their professional qualifications. People said to me, "Your husband has a Ph.D. and you only have a Masters. Why don't you use his papers when you apply for a job?" But I couldn't do that. It was wrong to do those things in a country which has taken us in. But I know that many people need work. They say they could drive a car and they buy a driver's license so that they can find work at once. I understand that they can't wait until they learn the language to take the proper test. There is a market for all kinds of paper in the Russian community. Green cards so people can work and other things like that.

Papers are of importance to all immigrants, particularly so for those who have lived in a country where papers were needed for daily activity. For the average American citizen, papers are of little importance: a driver's license, a birth certificate, a Social Security card are viewed as replaceable documents, easy to obtain. Indeed, there is a sense of entitlement to the possession of such papers. Realization of this came while standing on a line at the immigration service with a newly arrived immigrant. When the clerk asked him to put his papers in a basket, sit down, and wait his turn, he looked at me and asked, "Can I trust her to return them to me?" An American in the same situation might gripe about the bureaucratic procedure, the length of the line, the inefficiency of the Civil Service, or even the misplacement of the proper files, but there is a trust that the papers will be returned rather than arbitrarily taken away.

The average Russian sees papers as a vital part of his identity. "You are not a person if you do not have papers" is a Russian expression with far-reaching innuendos. Entitlement is often decided in arbitrary fashion by governmental agents: one must have the "proper" papers for a move from apartment to apartment, job to job, and city to city, and for marriage and retirement. The source of all paper dispersal is the government bureaucracy. But unlike the grumbling against bureaucratic delay and inefficiency carried on by Americans about other Americans in bureaucratic posts, in the USSR there is a fear of causing official displeasure to those who have the power to limit your access through the denial of papers of any sort.

M.D. relates that even when she and her family were packing their belongings and preparing to immigrate, the importance of papers was brought home to her.

> We threw away all of L.'s schoolwork because we did not have room to pack it to bring here. [The lady in charge of the apartment house] found them in the garbage and came rushing upstairs. "Why do you throw out those papers? They are important. You will be no loss to this country. It is good you are leaving. Imagine having no respect for such important documents that you can dispose of them so easily. Good riddance to the likes of you.

L.B. relates how, when she was expecting a package to be delivered, she had to provide the proper papers to the post office in order to get it:

> I got a notice that I had to come down and get a package from the United States. I came there without the piece of paper. I had traveled all the way there and now, even though they had the package and my name, they said I had to get the permission of the official in charge in order to get my package. He said I had to go home to get the proper paper and they would send someone to my house in order to check that I was the right person. I went home and when he came I told him that I knew that they only wanted me to pay them so that I could get the package and I would not be blackmailed in that fashion. They gave me a hard time. But I guess I scared them also, because in the end I got the package.

Having grown up with a respect for bureaucratic papers, even those who do not engage in major criminality have arrived with the ability to circumvent bureaucratic dealings through the paid intervention of people who produce the desired results without resorting to bureaucratic agency personnel. Other Russian immigrants have borrowed papers for entry, switched passports, and so on; but the growth of bureaucracy in this country and the bureaucratic nature of the home country of recent Russian immigrants has created fertile soil for a major enterprise in paper manipulation.

DOCUMENT FORGERY

This new immigration has brought to these shores people who made a living in the USSR doing forgery and reproduction. They have continued to make their living here doing the same, even for those who later move on to the world of the legitimate citizen. The academic diploma produced or reproduced as a job reference, the driver's license reproduced for display at the Motor Vehicle bureau as proof of driving skill (and immediate access to a New York License without a test)--these are the lesser criminal areas of paper manipulation. J.S., an American who lives in Brighton Beach, describes how this impressed him:

> The American police must be so stupid. It took them so long to catch up to the idea that the Russians couldn't even drive. Here in Brighton they are driving on the wrong sides of the streets, knocking over fire hydrants, hitting telephone poles, and no one even questioned the fact that they had come here without ever being behind the wheel. All they did was pay $500 for a Russian license and then they were able to get one here. I don't understand how the police work here. They are so innocent, and they don't even figure out what is going on.

Detective J.C. describes the case of the owner of M. I. International, the large food market in Brighton, who was indicted and convicted of selling phony Russian licenses: "They bought them so they could take them to Motor Vehicle and say they drove in the USSR." He states that driver's licenses are not the only forgeries involving new Russian immigrants: "They forge anything and sell it: counterfeit money, traveling papers, passports--anything. And the Russians seem to buy these things because there is a market in it."

Paper manipulation extends throughout the new Russian immigrant community. There is a buyer, a maker, and a seller of forged paper. There is the person who needs work and has to get a driver's license in order to move on to a legitimate activity, and there is a person who forges passports, green cards, and credit cards. For some, the making of papers was a professional activity worthy of respect in the USSR. For others, the purchase of papers serves only to affirm a necessity: the way to help parents leave the USSR, and perhaps the way to reach optimum employment possibilities in the United States.

S.R. and his family have been in the United States for four years. For almost all of that time he has been engaged in trying to bring his parents into this country. Because his exit from the USSR was granted on the understanding that he was going to Israel, he keeps trying to get his parents invited to visit someone else here in the United States. He believes that the Russian government thinks he still resides in Israel. His wife says that this idea is silly, because the Russian government knows exactly where each of its former citizens lives. In any case, in order to get his parents the correct papers of invitation, S.R. is involved with an agency set up by ex-Russian citizens, which is expected to prepare the "right" papers for his parents' invitation. He has had to pay large sums of money to this agency and has as yet had no results other than constant refusal, on the part of the Russian authorities, of all invitations issued to his parents.

L.B., another Russian immigrant, describes the many doctors practicing under the auspices of the American medical community and questions whether they were really doctors in the USSR. "Maybe they were," she says, "but there is so much false identification here in this community, who knows?"

So widespread is the manipulation of paper in this Russian community that it creates changes in the life-styles of those who wish not to be involved in illegal activities. An example of this was given to me by M.D., who described the following conversation with her doctor, also a recent Russian immigrant and presently resident of Brighton Beach:

> I see Doctor X in a clinic. But I know that he also has a private practice in a small office, which he opened recently. I asked him how this private practice was going. He told me that he had decided to close his office and limit his practice to the hospital clinic and to two nursing homes where he works as a relief doctor. I asked him why, because previously he had indicated that his private office was a satisfying and interesting practice. He told me the following reasons for closing his office: "*Shantazh* was the reason why I closed my office. They would come to me and ask me to give them a paper saying that they could not come to work because they were ill. That way they could collect government benefits. I did not want to do these kinds of things but they threatened me with *Shantazh* if I didn't. It became too frightening for me to have to deal with these people all the time, so I closed my office.

R.S., a woman from Brighton who immigrated within the past five years, describes her fear of reprisal and of *shantazh* when she describes why she does not sue the owner of a store in which she fell and suffered a foreshortened arm after treatment:

> The are all bad people in that store. They have a way of dealing with people. Maybe I could have collected something from the hospital for the poor treatment they gave me, but at the time I did not know enough to even think of suing. But I would never even tell the store owners that I got injured on

their property. They stood around and laughed at me when I fell, and they would just laugh at me if I approached them. They know too much about each one of us.

Chart 2 in Ch. 4 was compiled through interviews and discussions with the new Russian immigrant. It defines the understandings necessary for survival in the USSR and compares these understandings to an ultimate substitution of values for life in the United States. From careful analysis of these interviews, it was possible to divide the population into survivors and connivers. For our purposes, the survivor (necessary criminal) elected to "beat the system" in the Soviet Union in order to live in a vastly corrupt system. Connivers elected to use the system to profit materially in the Soviet system. They were concerned with more than survival; rather, they enjoyed the good life by engaging in criminal activity. Our interest here is in just how these value systems translate upon immigration.

It must be understood, however, that there are many new Russian immigrants whose sense of morality or whose religion precludes them from taking part in activities that they themselves understand to be immoral and wrong. These people comprise a good part of the new immigration. In no way can this research be interpreted to indicate that each and every new Russian immigrant is involved in criminality or accepts criminal actions as normal and correct.

The category of survivors that appears first in Chart 2 is of those who, as one of my informants described them, were the "real heroes" of the Soviet system: those who managed somehow to live their lives within a corrupt system while still managing to maintain their distance from this corruption, through some sort of personal ability or choice.

J.P., a woman who emigrated from Leningrad, describes these real heroes as people who live outside of the communist system: "the communist system is immoral. You constantly have to get. When people think about bread, clothes, and things like that they don't have the opportunity to think about life. Your mind is occupied with little things. Dissidents live on a higher level. They are not interested in obtaining things."

These are the people who, when they emigrate, find it most difficult to understand why our government is unable to deal with those of their compatriots who continue their Soviet behaviors after immigration. As S.R. says, "They come here and just do the same things they did there, but better."

It is hard to summarize the significance of these "dissidents." Their sense of morality prevented them from corrupt participation in the Soviet system, but they were aware that they had made a choice. They are also system beaters, but their way of system beating was different from that of their compatriots. Still they have the understandings that come from living in a system where, to get things done, one must get involved in the understandings that surround them.

Part of these people's understandings is their sharpened awareness of nuances and situations. Throughout my dealings with new Russian immigrants, I was aware that I was being asked to partake in their interpretations of particular situations through a nonexplicit system of understandings.

In describing her co-worker at the Hermitage, J.P. described the skills necessary for some of these interpretations: "We all had training in observations. She was trained to watch her co-workers and we trained ourselves to watch her. She reported on us and we knew we had to behave in such a fashion so she would report on nothing important. We exchanged looks, not words, and we understood." She tried to explain the kind of constant wariness that this type of existence entails: "We were always watchful. We were never sure who was around. We worked with the national heritage at the Hermitage. We could make money with it and some did. But we could be accused at any time."

All of those interviewed agreed that their lives in the USSR had trained them to be constantly vigilant. They were never sure when they were on safe territory, except in their most personal family relations. With others, except the most intimate friends, they watched, weighed, and were cautious. These understandings have been brought to their lives in the United States. M.D., a Russian immigrant, describes how caution is evident in dealings between Russian immigrants:

> Two years ago we were in a house of new Russians. We kept quiet. They kept quiet. We met again after a year and we started to talk. My friend, who had introduced us and was with us both times, said, "Why do you talk to each other now?" I said, "Last time they thought we were spies." We all started to laugh and agree to that. But I did not say that I thought they were spies also, which was why I had kept quiet. We are all still suspicious. We lived there in communal apartments. If the government didn't look at you, your neighbor looked at you.

Meeting any new Russian immigrant reaffirms their ability to "size you up." Unlike the average American, who might upon first meeting determine the class or the educational level of a stranger and then decide either to continue a conversation or not, according to need or desire, the new Russian immigrant makes the same determination with an added dimension. That dimension, born from a lifetime of experience, is fear. The new Russian immigrant seems to have developed a particularly sensitive antenna for evaluation of strangers, one that is unnecessary for the average American.

When I was first introduced to M.S. and Y.S. at a social occasion, they had no idea that I spoke Russian. Their English, although poor, was adequate for social conversation. We talked about the person who had introduced us, the fact that we were enjoying the social occasion at which we were meeting, and my admiration for their ability with the English language after so short a time in the United States. It was when I switched into Russian that I noticed the wariness. Now they did not know what to do with me or who I was or why I had this ability. I could see the dismissal in their eyes and shortly afterwards in their words. They turned to another person in the crowd, talked in their broken English and almost completely ignored me. I was a representative of the unknown and therefore of the threatening. They did not know why I had been introduced to them and what my interest was in them. They were unable to "size me up" from their life experiences; therefore I was a threat and they wanted nothing to do with me. Their experiences had suggested to them that I was there only because of them. My Russian-language ability in a room where there were supposed to be only Americans was threatening.

Several months after this encounter, and when we had become friends, they explained that their prior experiences in the USSR had taught them that someone as out of place as I was created for them an immediate fear. I was either a representative of the U.S. government, who was trained to speak Russian and could present a threat, or I was in some way part of the KGB, which most Russians in this country still fear (and which they believe is actively involved in new Russian immigrant activities). In either case, their experiences had taught them to turn away, to avoid, to disclaim.

It takes many years of reinforcement to begin to dispel the Russians' heightened awareness of nuances and situations, which they have been socialized to accept as part of life. I learned that in order to deal with Russian strangers, I had to begin by telling them a great deal about me, about my parents, about why I spoke Russian, about the fact that I had visited their home country, and about my understanding of how difficult it is to deal with strangers. Even then, I found that I caused a wariness in these people, as their perception of danger rose.

I spoke with C.C., a man who builds interiors for those who have stores in the Brighton Beach area. I talked to him about how life in this country compared to life in the USSR. He was open in his responses. "Life is hard for an old man who has to start over." We agreed that he was fortunate because he had skills that were needed on the open market. He explained that he was a designer and a craftsman, that he made a good income doing interiors for stores and nightclubs. When my questions suggested that I was interested in who owned some of the stores that were now so decorously rebuilt, I saw a glaze come over his eyes. "Well," he said rather rudely, "I have to get back to work now." I noticed that he stood outside the restaurant where we had been talking for over fifteen minutes apparently waiting for a ride. But his interest in me and in my questions had been turned off with a question into an area that for him suggested an occasion for wariness and interpretation of my role. To some extent this kind of heightened awareness is visible in people who populate the prisons of this country. They too respond to questions with the kinds of answers they feel are safe. But the average American citizen is not involved with this kind of interpretation of nuances and situations, whereas the new Russian immigrant is.

NOTES

1   Philadelphia Police report (unpublished).

2   Ibid.

3   "Lives of 2 Soviet Families Here," The New York Times, 4 September 1977.

4   Found in reports from New York, Philadelphia, Miami, etc.

5   New York City Police Department report (unpublished).

CHAPTER 6

Survivors and Connivers

Russians in the USSR have a heightened fear of being accused of committing criminal actions. Such accusations were often arbitrary in nature and therefore hard to prevent through positive actions. Awareness of the possibility of such accusations allowed for the kind of interpretations of nuances and situations that made for the heightened awareness of the new Russian immigrant. Therefore, Chart 2 (in Chapter 4), which begins on the left-hand side with the designation "necessary criminal," has to be viewed as a scale of such designation. All Russian immigrants interviewed agree that to exist in the system in the USSR, one is usually somehow involved in some sort of activity that could be arbitrarily designated by someone in authority as "criminal." Therefore, almost anyone immigrating from the USSR could be characterized as a "necessary criminal."

NECESSARY CRIMINAL THERE, SYSTEM BEATER HERE

As Chart 2 shows, those who were survivors in the USSR tend to remain so in the United States, and those who were engaged in criminal conniving tend to continue that activity here. To quote J.P., a recent Russian immigrant:

[All Russians] understand even better than Americans how to "make it." No family was untouched by war. They were trained for survival at every turn of Russian life. They are survival oriented and do what is necessary to survive. They are trained in observation. "You watch him and I'll pay you" is a part of their life on every job, in every apartment house, in every community.

Noncriminal system beaters there differ from American system beaters in a few respects. Here they try to make their family's life more comfortable through any device available. They use public funds, welfare, food stamps, to help them get started in life in this country. This very approach to these governmental benefits differs from that of the Americans because they have come from a system where there is an expectation of governmental funding. When I asked A.E. about taking welfare and working, she replied, "The government knows that people do this. Welfare is a good help to people. They come here naked, with nothing--although some do take advantage of the system." When questioned about the reason that the new Russian immigrants accept welfare, she explained that these immigrants have come from a system where there is no fear of unemployment. She explained that although it was hard to "live on one's 'allotment' in the USSR," there is no fear of that allotment's not coming in. The word "allotment," which refers to what we call "salary," has changed as the system of government in the USSR has changed. The former term for salary was *"zhalovanye."* The term is now *"zarplata."* A.E. explained the new Russian's understanding about accepting welfare in this fashion: "Well, the Russians see it as insurance, sort of an insurance policy, a kind of support. You see, they are afraid of losing a job so they take Medicare for their kids' sakes. In the USSR no one is afraid of losing jobs, but here how would you live?" I inquired whether there was fear of being caught doing what A.E. indicated she understood to be "somewhat outside of the legality." In answer to my question: "Aren't these people afraid that they will get caught?" she replied, "Yes. No. Not really. The government knows that people are doing this and they see it as a way to help people get themselves set up and that eventually they wouldn't need it. So they don't really do anything about it. They have to know about it. They allow it."

In effect, A.E. sees the U.S. goverment as a benevolent big brother who makes decisions, which it does not necessarily reveal, about its citizen's welfare. An example of this is the attitude with which she views "welfare cheating." Since enforcement is neither constant nor consistent, she says that she assumes the government has made a policy decision to allow it. She also discussed her perceptions of the "government view" of cash business: "The government knows that taxes are very high and people can't get started if they pay such high taxes. So it looks away and permits people to build a nest egg."

S.R. described another activity she considered prevalent in the Brighton Beach area--the large amount of coercion used by some members of the community against others:

> Another thing is like this: I have a business which I own in partners with someone else. I run it and decide that it is not doing well and I want to sell it. I say to my partner I don't have enough money to pay you back. He contracts with someone to come and force me to give him the money through threats and other things.
>
> And also, the kind of criminal things they all do have to do with taking advantage of the government. For example, I have a store. I tell the government that my daughter owns the store. If she is employed that way she doesn't collect from the government anyway. I can get welfare, pensions, SSI, Medicaid, shoes every six months, medicines. See, [the Russians] say to themselves, the Americans are stupid. If they give, why shouldn't I take? And so they go about their lives so that they can collect everything while they are also engaged in all kinds of business--legal and some illegal.
>
> Some say the United States owes us. My daughter works and her husband works. So they have to pay taxes. Their taxes pay for my pensions, my Social Security, my Section 8, everything. Very few people in Brighton work and do honest labor on which they pay their share. Most have a scheme or a racket of some kind. And that is if not actually engaged in thievery, drugs, and forgery of things.

In summary, the "necessary criminal there--system beater here" (NCT-SBH) sees law-enforcement agencies as ineffective. This type tries to measure these agencies, whether they are police and FBI or welfare and housing, against a measuring stick created from experience with similar arms of government in the USSR. These people have not found that our system creates the same threats of enforcement that they encountered in their home country. A major report issued by the Philadelphia police department cites among the major problems in dealing with the new Russian immigrant the "feeling among criminal element[s] that democratic societies [*sic*] law enforcement agencies are soft, inept and inefficient."[1]

As a result of experiences in their home country, the NCT-SBH weigh their experiences with these arms of the government against a social system that provided a certain amount of stipends as part of their "living" in the USSR. They look for similar benefits in the United States and some, particularly the older immigrants, see these benefits as a right. Others use these benefits as a way to establish themselves in legitimate jobs or as a supplement to the income they get from legitimate employment.

In order to cash in on many of the benefits available in the social system of this country, new immigrants may resort to being legal-paper violators. To this end they may purchase through illegitimate channels the papers necessary for proof of entitlement. In addition, the NCT-SBH may justify such purchases by claiming they are illegitimate steps toward attainment of legitimate ends, such as employment, in the case of purchased drivers licenses.

Finally, the NCT-SBH have a heightened awareness of the nuances and the situations in which they live. They bring with them a cultural baggage suggesting that they have to be constantly vigilant and ever watchful in their dealings with others. They interpret situations and the persons in these situations through the experience they brought from the USSR. This results in a climate of heightened awareness, compared with that of the typical American.

CRIMINAL THERE, SYSTEM BEATER HERE

This category in the new Russian community is the one that is most difficult to define. Informants' responses vary as to how many of their Brighton community businessmen are totally legitimate and how many are not. One group of respondents feels that many who were committing illegal actions in the Soviet Union, such as speculation--which is a crime there--are merely doing legitimate business here. Speculation is defined as profiting from the sale of merchandise. Thus, if one buys a sweater in the USSR for $1, and sells it for $5, he is guilty of a crime. Many of my informants feel that people who were skilled in the illegal manipulation of merchandise in the USSR can do the same thing here in legitimate business areas. Patrolman S. says:

> I don't think that the mom and pop operations along Brighton Beach are involved in doing criminal things. I think they may have started working for some of the mobs as couriers, or as waiters in their nightclubs and restaurants. But the mob seems to let them go when they wish and many of them have gone into their own businesses. They work long hours and make a living for themselves and their families.

P.B., a community worker whose organization works with these new immigrants, says that they work hard, put in long hours, and move up the economic ladder through diligence and persistence: "They are like every other group of immigrants. Of course they are aggressive. That is what they need to succeed. But they are succeeding very fast."

M.S., a recent Russian immigrant, discussed the fact that many of those who came to Brighton had been in business in the USSR. "If you know how to speculate and build up profits there, you do it even better here." She suggests that some of those who came brought money that enabled them to start businesses:

> T. was the director of a small store for the repair of TV. He controlled parts and distribution of some of these parts. He was able to trade off services for goods and he was able to do favors for people. So he had a great deal of money when he left. He came with furniture and maybe even some things in the furniture which helped him to start life here. And he was "slick" here, too. But he opened a store here and now he owns real estate and has some employees also.

R., a very articulate Russian immigrant, discusses the fact that there are people whose immigration eased their business problems, but they face problems of dealing with "imported" crime: "Here you can do business without paying off everybody. Except I've heard rumors that many of the Russian criminals here, who had no specialty there, are after some of those who are trying to do business in a perfectly legal fashion. They are trying to get in on schemes which threaten the legitimate businessman." Another informant feels that these very same businessmen, although engaged in legitimate enterprises, have antilegal values. Although they work hard, they are also willing to profit from illegitimate actions. Some are on the public dole while running their businesses under absentee names. Thus, they are able to collect under Section 8, which pays subsidy on their apartments, and welfare and food stamps, which supplement their legitimate incomes. Yet a lesser suspicion of illegality seems to come from those Americans who have contact with Brighton's immigrant community. These people, many of whom are community workers supplying services and social support to Brighton's Russians, do not find this population far different from other immigrants they have heard about.

P.B., an American who works at a community agency, (one interested in the total community of Americans and Russians rather than just new immigrants) suggests that some agencies prefer not to discuss the real situation in terms of extralegal activities because this type of discussion would jeopardize their sources of funding. P.B. said, "Look, we have to agree that this is a very aggressive population. But most of us have our jobs because of this population. We need it as much as it needs us." Yet after several hours of discussion, he did begin to refer to some of the population as being involved in extralegal activities: "That there is a criminal element is not fully substantiated. Maybe there is a minority criminal element here. It is shameful to the rest of the population because in some degree it impacts their activities."

Members of the Russian immigrant population tend to describe a much larger amount of criminal activity than do those who are not Russian, and they describe a great amount of illegality in their own immediate group. R.B., a new Russian immigrant who lives in Brighton, says that there is such a large amount of extralegal behavior that she began to wonder why she was so different from her neighbors and why she was not able to ease her life in the same manner as do others:

> I wonder why we don't do these things too. There are some people who live here and earn more money than we do but they don't pay the rent the way we do. They have number 8 [Section 8]. They have stamps and they get other kinds of help. We do it all alone. I would love to get out of this place but we can't afford to move and we can't bring ourselves to do some of the criminal things others do.

S.R., a Russian immigrant, says that many criminal activities go on in the Brighton Beach neighborhood of which the new Russian population is very much aware. With their sharpened awareness to nuances and situations, they have watched others in order to determine whether they are friend or foe. With these skills and understandings they are also able to determine who is involved in activities in the neigbhorhood and who is not. S.R. tells of the presence of a wide variety of criminal activities in her immediate neighborhood and of the semipublic character of these activities:

> More than 50 percent of the people who live in Brighton are engaged in criminal things. Fifth, Sixth and Seventh Streets--especially 3901 Fifth Street--are occupied almost completely by criminal families who are engaged in many bad things [*plokhiya veshchi*]. The most common element in all of them is that they collect from the government. There is an apartment on Seventh and another on Z where they sell stolen things. You can go up there and get what you need. You can go up there and make arrangements to have things stolen on order. For instance, you like a dress in a particular window. You don't want to pay, for instance, the $100 that it costs. So you make arrangements to have someone steal it for you for an arranged price. On Twelfth Street and on Second there are jewelry stores set up which handle only stolen merchandise.

R. says that "the ordinary citizen of the USSR is aware that the norms vocalized by society are far different from the norms adhered to by society." This is true of the new Russian immigrant in Brighton, too. R.S., a recent Russian immigrant, describes the attitude of some of the new Russian population that permits them to do illegal activities, and he argues that some illegality is necessary as a defense against even greater illegalities. "We need to forge a driver's license so we can work, not steal."

R.M., another new immigrant, relates how he came here as a professional house painter. He was hired by another Russian immigrant who had come several years earlier and had set himself up with a contracting business here. R.M. says that the contractor now has a union shop and works for large housing companies on a contract basis, but he employed R.M. for over two years as a nonunion painter. R.M. explains that there is a limitation on the amount of weeks a nonunion painter can work for a union shop, but it proved to be no problem since he worked under a variety of names and was shuttled around from team to team during this time. He was eventually hired in proper fashion and now works legitimately and feels that he earns a good living.

In R.M.'s case, "criminal" illegality was a transitional phase to legality. In fact, he is now quite disturbed that in the Brighton community so many people live who are involved with the rackets, with evasion, with deception of all governmental services. He finds it upsetting that he pays full rent and asks no help of any sort while all around him are so many people who are "stealing from the government and from each other."

Still, the legitimate businessman, as well as the system beater, looks to the government as a major source of largesse, whether legal or illegal. They become familiar with the bureaucratic manipulation needed to comply with the necessary standards for qualification for the various governmental subsidies available, whether they be HEAP grants, Section 8, or Medicaid and welfare. But they have little respect for governmental paper or qualification standards. Thus they employ bureaucratic entrepreneurial skills in both the legal and the illegal areas of business.

Those who are a part of the new Russian community and those Americans who deal with this community agree that the new Russian population tends to hide money rather than deposit it in banks. In the USSR money in the bank was an indication that one was obtaining money through means other than employment. Thus, in the United States, this population tends to find other ways to deal with money. For one thing, they invest and deal in real estate. J.S., an American community leader, describes how this has affected the local real estate market:

> They made a great effect on the real estate market in Brighton. Since they have been here that market has changed. Rentals have tripled in the past four years. That is the best way to hide cash. They give $2,000 bribes to superintendents, and some families own eight, nine apartments. They sublet, get in on HEAP grants and purchase businesses and homes for cash. People in Brighton are paying $90,000 for houses which cost $40,000 two years ago.

P.S., an American actively involved in community activities in Brighton, states that in the past two years a large number of new stores have opened in the community. She sees these as an indication that the local residents have worked hard, saved their money, and are now able to start their own businesses. "I think there may have been investments that they were involved in which were not quite legitimate also," she says. Money can also be used for lending, with a high return in interest.

P.B., also an American, suggests that this is a hard-working group that uses whatever means are available to set itself up in a path leading to success in the American system: "After a while they realize that they are doing harm working off the books. We tell them that they have no references and that will not be a help in the future. But you have to remember that the people who come to us ask for help. There are many others who manage themselves."

It is those who manage by themselves that provide an example of initially subverting a system in order to become a part of the system. Those people who in the USSR were involved in illegal speculation can come here and at first manipulate the bureaucratic agencies to provide themselves with financial support with which to begin their rise up the economic ladder. They also speculate in real estate and usury and are involved in initial subversion of the legal codes in an attempt to reach a position where further subversion may no longer be necessary. The very entrepreneurial skills which they were able to use for profit, albeit illegally, in the USSR, they can now use for profit, legally, in the United States.

Police statistics, of course, do not reflect unreported crimes. Therefore, the official statistics for the 60th Precinct (Brighton Beach) reflect less criminal activity than that indicated by my informants. Police statistics are not able to reflect accurately the actual crime because in some ways that crime is invisible. In a population that distrusts the police, fewer people report crimes to the police. In a population trained to remain uninvolved, fewer crimes are "seen." In this Russian population, there is a long-ingrained habit of not dealing with governmental agents of any sort, if such dealings can be avoided. In addition, there is justifiable fear of retribution for making police reports. Thus, the community tends to retain as secrets its knowledge of crime.

There is in the Brighton Beach population, however, a general awareness of the criminality in the area and a knowledge of the large amount of violence that seems to touch every family, if only because of their fear of that criminality. The police and my informants agree that this is an armed community. Both legitimately, with licenses, and illegitimately, through easy access, many members of the community are armed. Storekeepers and citizens who work in other areas belong to target-shooting clubs (or so they claim) in order to obtain licenses.

R.S., a recent immigrant, describes this awareness as follows:

All the businessmen around here have pistols. They are all afraid of crime. They are afraid of the Russians and they are afraid of others. People are killed here and the small store owners are becoming armed. Even my husband carries a pistol. But his is a gas gun, although it has a place for bullets. Some get licenses but some just buy the guns where they are sold in Brighton. Yes, I know where.

R.B. describes how, in a two-week period, he was aware of two violent incidents:

The three of them had a falling out. How do you say it? We say a falling out of thieves. One was shot two times in the stomach. Another was stabbed, and the third was beaten up badly. But the police don't know about it because no one talks.

No, they didn't go to the hospital. Someone here in the community took out the bullets.

On another evening we were invited to a restaurant. There was a fight in the restaurant and we left. But the following morning everyone was talking about the fight. One person was taken by ambulance to the hospital but somehow no one knows who did it.

A plain-clothes detective described the kinds of activities which occur in the Brighton Beach area as follows: "Since 1978, crime in this area has increased greatly. There used to be incredible amounts of burglaries. These have been reduced since merchants have become heavily Russian and know who to look for. Also there are some hints of protection rackets." He went on to describe a social club that operates on the boardwalk and suggested that it is not even a safe place to walk past: "I wouldn't even look in the door if I were you. There is a large amount of violence which goes on there: beatings and knifings. I think a large amount of the population is not Jewish. I think that when they opened the doors a lot of people ran out with false papers and in any way they could." He described much of the population as a "rough crowd," involved in quite a bit of "fighting, shootings, and stabbings."

A police report describes the specific criminal activities of this population as varying from homicide, narcotics, and robbery through extortion, arson, and fencing. This report defines the Brighton Beach area as a "Major Problem Area" of criminal activity among the new Russian population. Because of the ability of this population to manipulate paper, counterfeiting is a specialty, including U.S. currency, gold coins, driver's licenses, passports, immigration cards, art works, and religious icons.[2]

L.B. pointed out a well-dressed man on Coney Island Avenue and suggested that I clutch my purse tighter: "Everyone knows him as a famous purse snatcher. Look at the way he is dressed. That is what he does--he pushes you and takes your purse." When asked what he does with the items in the purse, L.B. pointed to several shops, explaining that they specialized in stolen goods. "And they deal with VISA cards too," she intoned.

CRIMINAL THERE, CRIMINAL HERE

As indicated in Chart 2 in Ch. 4, there is a cumulative effect as one moves further down the right side of the chart, with each group in some ways encompassing those activities of the previously described group but adding other, more specific criminal activities. Thus, the category NCT-SBH has a sharpened awareness of nuances or situations, but so does the "criminal there--criminal here" (CT-CH). It is the added activities under each new category that distinguish the persons in that category.

It has to be acknowledged that as of yet, one has to rely on informants who are not involved in the specific activities described, or on law-enforcement personnel who are just at the beginning of their education about this community. The education of the law-enforcement community comes about because of specific acts reported to them by victims. This kind of reporting is particularly ineffective in gaining understanding of a self-contained and foreign-speaking community like the new Russian community of Brighton Beach. My information, then, is based on discussions with members of this community, who see "bad" things going on all around them (but report what they see).

Los Angeles has been aware through its police department and subsequent reports in the press of a growing criminal problem aggravated by new Russian immigrants:

> The Soviet Union has infiltrated spies and criminals into the United States for the apparent purpose of aggravating America's growing crime problems, Los Angeles Police Chief Daryl Gates charged today.
>
> Gates disclosed that the "Russian Emigre Mafia" members entered the United States under the guise of being dissident Soviet Jews escaping religious oppression in their homeland. "We have, indeed, identified some who are not Jews coming in under this quota and who have been involved in criminal activity," Gates said.[13]

The article quotes Gates as saying that the Los Angeles criminal group is "controlled and directed from the Brighton Beach area of Brooklyn, N.Y."[4] An article in *New York Magazine*, February 16, 1981, is entitled: "Are Soviets Sending Misfits Here?" and suggests that the Soviet Union is "using this country as a dumping ground for the violent and antisocial."[5]

Among the new Russians,there is some talk of the population of Odessa, specifically of an area called Moldavanka, which has settled some of its citizens in Brighton. This area has for generations been the marketplace of Odessa. Like similar areas in other metropolises, Moldavanka housed not only the poorer classes but also those involved in various scams and marginal activities. In addition, since Odessa is a port, there is a stream of sailors moving through the area always ready to buy or sell whatever is available. For generations this has been an area where one could fence or buy stolen goods and obtain forged papers. M.D. has suggested to me that "when the doors opened up, many on the verge of being caught ran through them."

ORGANIZED AND STRUCTURED CRIMINAL ACTIVITIES

Several areas of uncertainty exist about this professionally criminal population. It is hard to determine whether there is an organized structure of the criminal activities that go on in Brighton Beach, and it is additionally hard to determine whether there is foreign (governmental) involvement in these activities. Because both of these questions raise fundamental issues about detection of criminal activities by agents of the police and the FBI, and because they themselves have not yet determined just how organized the criminal activity is, it is worthwhile to pursue both of these questions.

In *The Challenge of Crime in a Free Society*, a report by the President's Commission on Law Enforcement and Administration of Justice (1967), organized crime is described as follows:

> Organized crime is a society that seeks to operate outside the control of the American people and their governments. It involves thousands of criminals, working within structures as complex as those of any large corporation, subject to laws more rigidly enforced than those of legitimate governments. Its actions are not impulsive but rather the result of intricate conspiracies, carried over whole fields of activitiy in order to amass huge profits.[6]

Since the latest immigrants have only recently entered the United States, law-enforcement agents are still trying to discover whether they are involved with an organized society directing criminal acts in order to amass profits. It will take much more contact with them and with their criminal element before an organized structure, if one exists, can be clearly ascertained. Structure is of special interest to law-enforcement agencies because it provides a means of control. Yet although Detective J.C. says that he has begun to chart a criminal structure within this population, he is unsure whether there are individual, separate families with ties and allegiances to each other, and whether there are enduring networks of criminals who knew each other in Russia and who work together here. The detective commented: "I've heard that they get involved in different things with different people and keep the money for themselves, but I've also been able to find relationships and tie-ins within those who have been caught. And also I have spotted them hanging out with each other, so that may mean that there is a structure. I don't know if it is families or what." Whether there is a hierarchy of control is, as of now, open to debate among those law-enforcement agents who deal with the new Russians. At a meeting with J.C. and P.G., representing two different law-enforcement agencies that deal with this population, we discussed the likelihood of a central structure. We discussed the "people's court" about which we had heard independently from several informants. This "court" is presumed to render judgments among disputing parties without resorting to the agencies of the legal system.

One must ascertain whether this "people's court" deals with matters only of criminal involvement or whether it is used to settle community disputes. If it deals with criminals and is used to settle their territorial or monetary disputes, then it can be a sign that there is a structured criminal community with a hierarchy of command "subject to laws" as is the case with organized crime. In the following incident, described to the police by Russian informers who know about the people's court, the court deals with criminals and makes determinations between criminal elements. Knowledgeable people describe the "judges" in this court as "important people within the community." As described to Detective J.C., the incident is as follows: "One individual demanded money from another individual. The one who had to do the paying said that he didn't think he had to pay. They requested a people's court. And they abided by its decision. Now both of these guys were known and big shots so the court must have some power."

A Russian immigrant who lives in the Brighton area agrees that the people's court is used by the "bad" people to settle their disputes and states that she will not even go into stores owned by some of those she knows are involved in the underworld activities of the area. She pointed out a large market and several nightclubs as businesses involved with "bad" people; but she vigorously denied that all the nightclubs were owned by bad people. To her, bad people were those who not only lived a criminal life here but had also lived a criminal life in the USSR. She saw them as a network of friends and families who maintain their relationships here in the same fashion as in the old country. Another Russian also agreed that they found each other apartments in neighboring houses and helped each other out in the same way that they had helped each other out before immigrating.

In addition, the Russians have mentioned that there are medical personnel in the community who render aid to those who do not go through the regular channels, i.e., those who cannot afford to have their wounds reported as a licensed physician would be legally obligated to do. This too substantiates the concept of a sublegal, semicriminal stratum in the community.

As more crimes are reported and as those who commit them are found to have organized connections to others who have been apprehended, there may be more information with which to determine accurately the amount of organization of the criminal network. At the moment, however, it appears that there is a gradation from single persons doing criminal acts to groups of interconnected criminals acting both in organized and in informal conjunction with others. However, a pattern of the same names is beginning to appear in the reporting of major illegal actions. The charting of these names in an attempt to establish organized patterns is only possible in a sketchy fashion so far.*

This population has, as Detective J.C. states, "learned to maneuver on our turnpikes." He describes how someone will fly to Cincinnati, go into a large department store, emerge with furs and other stolen items, and then fly back to New York to fence them:

> Any Soviet immigrant collared for resisting arrest, kicking cops, beating on other people, or using bats on others, has started out with shoplifting. They will get on a plane, fly to another city, fly back, and fence. The flea markets in certain locations on Brighton's Surf Avenue all have fencing operations. It's called hooliganism by the Russians. But it is very much inbred. They know how to manipulate the system very well and to find the weak points of our system.

M.B., a Russian immigrant, describes the pattern of a man she had known in the USSR:

> He was a thief there. When he left, the day after he left, they came to arrest him. But he had paid for documents to get out. He went to Israel and then to Italy. He was involved in narcotics there. My daughter had grown up with him and she found him again here in New York. He was robbing again

---

*Conversations with the Russian specialists within the Intelligence Division of the Organized Crime Monitoring Unit of the New York City Police Department and the Russian specialist at the Joint Organized Crime Task Force of the FBI confirm that the question of discerning organized patterns is at the very embryonic stages.

and he had diamonds and gold. He went back with them to Germany. He married again there. His first wife he had left in the USSR together with his young daughter. They could not follow him because the government wanted them to leave all their things, their furniture. They had beautiful things and a wonderful apartment, but the government said all this was "owed to them" because the husband had escaped. So they stayed. He got married again and he travels the whole world. Everyone from Odessa knows him. His name is Fema and he was a famous thief there.

Law-enforcement sources, both national and international, are confirming to each other the fact that an unusual number of Russian emigres are involved in felony charges in a multiplicity of jurisdictions. Much of the activity is directed against members of the Jewish population, although in recent months, activities have spread into the general community.

Detective J. C. describes the multiplicity of criminal activities engaged in by several prominent families in the Brighton Beach area. However, these activities are not limited to the area of residence, but occur in cities throughout the country. He described how, after a suspect was arrested for arson, he was found to be involved in a number of other crimes:

On his person we found two checks for $100 each. Also on him we found the wallet and in it the license of another Soviet immigrant, and those checks signed in that other person's name. We found that he had no green card on him, only those two checks which were part of $4,000 in traveler's checks which were reported stolen from a guy going to Club Med. His license was also reported stolen by a lady who turned out to be an associate of the one who reported these things stolen. She was also a Russian immigrant.

She didn't know the guy we arrested. But she was paying $49 for a $4,000 apartment. We figured out that these arsonists had another guy's license and all three had arrived into this country together. These stories get very complicated because they use all sorts of stolen papers and often change names and their prints do not match up.

Another case cited by Detective J.C. involves a jewelry store recently opened by a group of new Russian immigrants:

Recently, in Franklin Square, Russians opened a jewelry store in a shopping mall. It was near another store owned by a long-time resident of the area. A male and female walked into the resident's store and showed him, the complainant, some jewelry. They asked him if he wanted to buy it and told him that it was very valuable. He said he didn't know anything about jewelry and they suggested that since there was a jewelry store in the same mall as his store, he should go there and ask their opinion. He took it to the jeweler and was told that, indeed, it was worth a lot of money. The jeweler said that since the male and female had wanted $70,000 for the jewelry and he knew that it was worth more, he would buy it from the complainant for $120,000 after he purchased it. He went back and forth several times and finally decided that he would do it. The deal goes down and when he goes back the jeweler knows nothing about it.

Now, the jeweler is related to the other guy's daughter. That makes him the brother-in-law of Shlomo, who is wanted all over the country for scams.

A news feature describes how two Franklin Square jewelers-- the same ones who had been involved in the crime just reported, claim they were robbed. The jewelers stated that they had been chained in the rear of their store while three men removed $12,000 in cash and jewelry of undetermined value. They stated that while they were showing engagement rings to a couple, another man rang the doorbell and was admitted. The two jewelers, whose names are familiar to the police because of their involvement in the previously described confidence game, stated that the three who robbed them emptied their cases of jewels, then left them unable to report the robbery. It is questionable whether there was indeed a robbery or whether there was a setup for some other sort of scam, either of an insurance company or of some unpaid account.[7]

This situation--a robbery reported by people who have already come to the attention of the police and who know that they have come to their attention--summarizes many problems involved in studying this population. Were the jewelers so naive that they assumed that the police would not connect the two crimes because they were committed at different times and under different agency investigations? Were the jewelers actually robbed? If so, was the robbery committed with their knowledge and consent, and were they to get part of the profits? Were they robbed because they owed a debt to some Russian hierarchy, if one exists? Did they profit or lose from this robbery?

It will take much more investigation before any of these points can be determined and before the existence of an organized criminal structure in the new Russian immigrant community can be confirmed. But indications are growing that the people involved in these many criminal activities know one another, and the same names, in relationship with others, repeatedly come to the attention of the authorities. Additionally, police and FBI agents are beginning to acknowledge the need for a major cooperative effort in order to document the population involved in these criminal activities.

The category of CT-CH needs further investigation. No preliminary study such as this can detail the many and varied types of
crimes among the new Russian population. One can only speculate.
Yet the emigres have presented to the law-enforcement agencies in
the United States and the rest of the Western world the spectacle
of an emerging criminal class. As yet it is undetermined how much
of this criminality is private organized crime and how much of it is
international espionage. That they interweave at some levels is a
possibility. That the population is skilled in deviant behavior from
years of maneuvering in the Soviet system is more apparent. It is
evident that in the Brighton Beach community a vast amount of at
least informally organized crime exists.

The Organized Crime Monitoring Unit has become a source of
information for other major city police departments, and Brighton
Beach contacts crop up in their reports. A police report of a major
Eastern city states:

> Numerous other investigations have been initiated in
> various parts of the country. These include: investigation into
> a group of Soviet immigrants by the United States Secret
> Service in regard to the counterfeiting of U. S. currency;
> numerous burglaries nationwide involving the theft of millions
> of dollars worth of Russian antiques and icons, a nationwide
> ring of antique and icon counterfeiters; the smuggling of U.S.
> currency into the United States; insurance frauds involving life
> insurance, homeowner and business insurance frauds and auto
> accident frauds in which the same Soviet immigrants are
> involved. Also, there are social security, welfare and IRS
> investigations underway.
>
> Further, it is reported that the FBI is actively engaged in
> an investigation concerning possible subversive activities
> involving these Soviet immigrants across the nation.
>
> In conclusion, it is evident that an organized criminal
> group exists within the Russian Immigrant community.
> Members of this group refer to themselves as the "Russian
> Mafia." It is a present and growing threat to our nation. Their
> obvious sophistication far exceeds that of La Cosa Nostra in its
> infant state.
>
> The "Russian Mafia" has perpetrated a series of crimes
> rivaling any of those perpetrated by existing organized
> criminal groups. It is imperative that a concerted effort be
> made by Federal, state and local law enforcement agencies to
> identify this group's leadership and membership as well as
> compile and maintain files on their activities.[8]

This attempt to catalog the population presents special problems to law-enforcement agencies. At this point, several "families" appear to surface, together with their minions, specializing in

criminal behavior. Reports from as far away as Winnipeg, Canada, where there is a large Russian emigre community, describe the same kinds of gold coin scams that are being carried on in many cities across the U.S. Whether these crimes are committed by the same persons, persons directed by a particular leader to commit these acts, or a variety of different people doing the same crime, has not as yet been definitely established.

KGB INVOLVEMENT?

In addition to attempted investigation into structure within the criminal population of the new Russian community, the question of continued Russian governmental involvement with this population remains unanswered. Many Russian immigrants maintain that the USSR would not have allowed so many people to emigrate without sending out some with whom it was able to maintain ties.

M.S., a Russian immigrant, discusses the amount of violence and crime that goes on in the new Russian community and concludes that the people who do it are not really truly part of the Jewish immigration: "They worked for higher-ups. They were involved in banditry [there]. That is, thieving for members of the Party. I never knew Jews who did that there. But when they come here they are still working for higher-ups. You don't think the KGB would let them go just like that. It would never pass up an opportunity like that." She explains that it is hard to determine who left the USSR because they saw better opportunities elsewhere and who left the USSR because they were told to for governmental purposes: "Of those who were involved in these things and worked for those in power, some may have taken the opportunity to leave when the gates opened and they ran. Others came on a mission."

J.P., a Russian woman who emigrated to the United States without experiencing any delay between application and immigration, attributes this to the fact that she was used as an instrument in the successful placement of one such spy:

At work everyone knew that she was reporting on all of us to the KGB. That was her job and she really didn't do any other job that much. I know that one of the reasons why it was easy for my family to leave Leningrad was because three people in my job were allowed to go at the same time. It was to get her out that we were permitted to exit also. When she got here we avoided her. She had been a spy there and we were sure that she would be here, too. But it is really funny. I was visited by the FBI. They came to investigate her. But not because of her spying. They were checking her references because she had gotten a job in the California language school run by the Army. She was to teach Russian there. Can you imagine?

All my Russian informants agreed that there was a subpopulation in the new Russian community that had been sent here with Soviet governmental ties. These informants, who grew up being watched and watching, are particularly sensitive to this issue. It is hard to determine whether these informants continue to see spies because they are so used to living with them that to be without them takes away some of life's importance, or whether indeed they are more perceptive concerning this particular aspect of the Russian emigration.

Unlike the new Russian immigrants, the various American agencies that deal with these new Russian criminals are not unanimous in their opinions about KGB involvement, although they do see the population as being involved in criminal activities of international scope. The FBI, and Customs and Immigration authorities, as well as various international law-enforcement agencies, are investigating worldwide crimes such as drug trafficking, jewel thefts, and monetary manipulations which have involved this Russian population.

A report of the Los Angeles Police Department describes the concerns emerging because of the known activities of members of this new Russian community. This report which discusses the fact that "some of these refugees were not Jewish, and were in fact criminals in the Soviet Union" predicts that this population will be used to embarrass the United States: "Predictable intelligence resources could have considerable impact upon the success of law enforcement's efforts during the Olympic Games. Currently very limited resources are available to deal with the Soviet emigre threat."[9]

This concern about the type of person who was sent out of the USSR is evident is an article in the *U.S. News and World Report* headlined, "New York City: Hotbed of Soviet Spies." Although the article is primarily about those members of the Soviet government who work in various diplomatic positions in New York, it also discusses the concept of "sleeper" spies:

> A new concern is the growing number of Russian emigres [then] arriving in New York by the hundreds each month. They concentrate in the Brighton Beach section of Brooklyn. Among these immigrants, it is believed, are some "sleeper" agents being planted here to meld into American life and later emerge as spies.
>
> "We know there are persons who got out of Russia only on their promise to cooperate when they get here," notes R. Jean Gray, head of the local FBI section that keeps an eye on Russians.
>
> Officials refuse to estimate how many such sleepers are secretly at work in the United States, but sources indicate that many are known to the FBI and are kept under quiet surveillance.[10]

Yet the criminal activities of this new Russian population has brought them to the attention of American local police departments, U.S. enforcement agencies, the police of various other Western nations, and to police agencies that provide cooperation on an international scale. In an article in *The New York Times* in February 1983, reference is again made to a Russian Mafia, although it does not clarify whether many of the crimes described are conducted on an international scale and in some ways contradict the previous quote as it concerns structure:

> "We don't yet know the full scope of their activities," said Mr. Murphy, who is in charge of the FBI office for Brooklyn, Queens, and Long Island, "but we do know they are growing fast and that they have been very successful. We're talking about staggering amounts of money, in the multi-million-dollar range."
> The "Russian Mafia," as some Brighton Beach residents call it, does not appear to have the sort of sophisticated structure that characterized traditional organized crime. You don't have the level of hierarchy," Mr. Murphy said. "But if it is allowed to keep growing at the rate it's growing now, it will be very well organized in the years to come."
> The spectrum of activities in which Russian organized crime is involved, according to law-enforcement officials and several sources in Brighton Beach, includes protection rackets, gambling, confidence schemes, counterfeiting, forgery and sales of licenses and travel documents, smuggling, burglary, armed robbery, drug and weapon sales, and murder.[12]

Mike Mallowe, writing in *Philadelphia*, describes an organization that he calls the "Malina," comprised of emigre Russians. He calls this organization a "new Mafia" and describes its European contacts as "extensive":

> It is an international criminal conspiracy that will engage in any crime, from murder to espionage to drug trafficking to jewel theft, for the right price. Up till now, many of its members entered this country as Soviet Jews and most of its victims have been from the emigre community. But the Malina is growing. It numbers the KBG and the CIA among its contacts, and perhaps its clients.
> The Malina was born in the Russian city of Odessa. Most of its members operated in the thriving black market that existed there. In the early 1960's, according to one top secret FBI analysis, members of the Malina began to emigrate from Russia to Israel, where they re-established their criminal network. Over the years these Israeli hoods branched out from Tel Aviv to other cities, including London, Paris, Antwerp,

Vienna, Rome, New York and Los Angeles. Some members of the Malina brotherhood really are Russian Jews. Others have merely purchased false identities of Russian Jews killed or imprisoned in the Soviet Union. They obtained forged visas and emigration permits. A handful of the men in the Malina are almost certainly KGB agents. Most, however, are first class international criminals. [13]

U.C., a New York City undercover detective, interviewed on the boardwalk in Brighton, described the international aspect of this population in terms of bringing in illegal immigrants through the cooperation of other members of the immigrant community:

There are people here who are not Jewish but they married Jews in order to get into the United States. Then they divorced, either in legal ways or just stopped living together, and moved in with other people. Also there is the Russian Mafia, an underworld population involved in international drug trade, diamonds and such. They all really know how to use our bureaucracy in order to gain access to government services, welfare, Section 8, and so on.

Detective J.C. described how a particular new Russian immigrant has been tracked through Europe and the United States and is presently engaged in several criminal activities, while still eluding the police.

S. was collared on the Thruway in Jersey for possession of a gun. It was discovered that when immigration gave him the print card to go get [finger] printed he uses another guy for the prints. Recently immigration discovered that it was not his prints. Then he was in Rome and was collared for traveler's checks. He could be right here in Brighton and he could be anywhere in the country. It is possible that when they go to Europe they have contacts with the KGB. West Germany has set up a criminal commission just to handle these complaints.

If one observes the process at immigration, where immigrants hand in their papers, then sit down with other "foreigners" to wait to be printed, it is possible to understand how substitutes can be enlisted to be printed instead of the person whose papers were presented. The room is crowded and there is the usual casualness encountered with American bureaucratic endeavors, an easy mark for Russians skilled in bureaucratic systems. There seems to be little reason to assume that these people who came here for asylum would not follow procedural rules. Yet this person and possibly others skillfully evaded the bureaucracy and established mixed identities.

A report of the Los Angeles Police Department speculates as follows:

> It is readily foreseeable that the crime problem involving Soviets will increase in size and severity. . . . Additionally, the Soviets apparently believe that the 1984 Olympic Games offer an opportunity to embarrass the United States. The Soviet news agency TASS has already characterized Los Angeles as crime-ridden and smog beset and has hinted some disaster might befall the Games.[14]

At present it appears difficult for police spokespersons to differentiate between (1) immigrants who continue to engage in criminal activities similar in nature to, or in elaboration of, those activities in which they engaged while in the USSR, and (2) immigrants who maintain ties not only to criminals in European cities but also to those in the USSR with whom they dealt before immigration. Knowledgeable people in the law-enforcement community agree that this new Russian group is a unique immigration. For one thing, this population comes from a bureaucratic society to one that, although not as bureaucratic, has similar elements. In addition, this group's criminals are older than those of other new immigrations. One expert--a detective with the Organized Crime Monitoring Unit of the New York City Police Department, assigned to the desk that deals with new Asian immigrants--compared the Russian group with the organized-crime subgroup among recent Asian immigrants, specifically, the Chinese. He found the two groups most dissimilar. For one thing, his main concern was with a young population, whereas the population involved in criminality in the Russian community is middle-aged, implying a criminal orientation that predated immigration. In addition, the Chinese criminal cadre retained its loyalties to the feuds of the ancient Tong societies. These criminals' heritage was still ruling their behavior. "They are members of the 'dark societies' of Tong distinction, the feudal lords." In addition, the detective saw no similarities in their views toward the state. He said that the Chinese population took very little subsistence from the government; they found bureaucratic involvement threatening and tried to avoid it. The Russians took the bureaucracy for granted and oriented their activity toward using it, manipulating but escaping it.

The Russian population characterized as "criminal there-- criminal here" is not only different from other immigrant populations from non-Communist countries, but in many ways it is also different from large segments of the criminal populations known here at similar stages of immigration. Their ability to commit their crime in one city, state, or nation and then to move on to another city, state, or nation is unique in the history of immigrant crime. Mobility, facilitated by cheap and easy access to transportation without complicated proof of status, allows this population to enlarge their territory in a way that we have not charted among earlier criminal populations.

It remains to be determined whether this particular Russian criminal, i.e., the one who is involved in major criminal activities on an international scale, or even just on a national scale, is part of a structured network. Additionally, it remains to be determined whether this criminal is controlled from within the USSR. These are two separate concepts: one suggests a Mafia-like structure based on previous association but uncontrolled by the political motives of another nation; the other suggests that there exists an overall control from a foreign power, which motivates a criminal element to serve, in part, its purposes. It is also possible that some of both exist. Indeed, we may all be touching different parts of the elephant and coming up with different analyses of just what kind of beast we have before us. We do know, however, that we have before us a criminal element with great mobility, with a national and international scope, involved in a multiplicity of criminal activities, with a possible KGB connection.

Time and further research are needed to begin to answer the many questions apparent in the study of this new Russian population.

NOTES

1 Philadelphia Police report (unpublished).

2 Ibid.

3 Gates, "Jews Make Peace on Emigrants." Los Angeles Times, 28 January 1982.

4 Ibid.

5 "Are Soviets Sending Misfits Here?" The New York Times, 16 February 1981.

6 The Challenge of Crime in a Free Society (U. S. Government Printing Office, Washington, D.C. 1967), p. 187.

7 "Jewelry Store is Held Up," New York Daily News, 19 January 1984.

8 Philadelphia Police report (unpublished).

9 Los Angeles Police Department report (unpublished).

10 "New York City: Hotbed of Soviet Spies," U.S. News and World Report, 18 January 1982.

11 Philadelphia Police report (unpublished).

12 "Russian Mafia in Brighton Beach," The New York Times, 14 February 1983.

13 Mike Mallow, "From Russia with Guns," Philadelphia Inquirer, May 1983.

14 Los Angeles Police Department report (unpublished).

CHAPTER 7

Previous and Current Immigrations

This book has focused on the new Russian immigrant in an attempt to determine whether certain cultural templates--specifically, understandings, behaviors, and actions with respect to crime-- change upon the immigration of their bearers. Specifically, this study has examined the Russian emigres who have arrived within the past decade and who reside in the oceanside community of Brighton Beach, Brooklyn. In this primarily middle-class community, many of the businesses are owned and operated by the new immigrant population.

These new immigrants are far different from those of the 19th and early 20th centuries, who are the focus of much of the literature about immigrants. The new Russian immigrants have arrived in the United States after living in a technological and bureaucratic society. They are primarily middle class and with marketable employment skills that are adaptable to the job market of this country. Their role in their old society is transferable to their role in ours. A house painter can paint houses everywhere, and an industrial sewing-machine mechanic can do the same work in either country.

I have partially attempted to examine sociological theories of immigrant adaptability as they might apply to new types of immigrants. Much of the literature about immigrants originated at a time when the United States was host to wave upon wave of new immigrations, often coming from countries where the level of

125

economic and industrial development lay far behind that of this country. The early immigrants described in the literature were marginally skilled agrarian workers or unskilled laborers, injected into a society where their ability to enter the job market was hampered by their relative lack of marketable skills.

I have looked at the new Russian immigrants against the background of their understandings, acquired after a lifetime of learnings in a country where there was technology, bureaucracy, and industrialization. The new immigrants were not similar to those reflected by the older literature, whose criminality was seen as necessary to ascend the American social ladder. On the contrary, the new immigrants come from a country where resorting to criminality is part of the lifetime of learning necessary for survival in the homeland. Of interest to us was whether the coping skills and techniques learned in the Soviet Union changed upon immigration to a country where these skills and techniques are less needed.

I disagree with much of the sociological literature, which suggests that immigrants learn the success ethic after immigration. The population studied here arrived in this country already honed by similar values in another society. In effect, the group I examined moved from one country to another--after having spent a lifetime of learning in the first country--in order to apply that learning after immigration.

Because of the understandings necessary for existence in the USSR, these immigrants are skilled in behavior needed for living in a particularly corrupt system of acquiring and dispensing goods and services. These skills were needed to journey through the avenues of corruption that are part of the daily ambience for most of the Russian population. Difficulties in acquiring the goods and services necessary to everyday life had taught this population that one had to operate outside and against the official channels of distribution. People relied primarily on friends, colleagues, and neighbors--but not the official agencies--to fulfill daily expectancies of life. Those who could obtain material goods had the ability to barter, bribe, and in other ways lighten the load on their lives and the lives of their families. Although aware that these everyday behaviors were outside of the legal system, the immigrants also knew that this type of behavior was the operating norm, carried on not only by people like themselves, but also by all those around them, as well as by those in minor and major positions of power. Indeed, as conventional wisdom had it, "Everyone was doing it."

"Doing it" and fear of being caught necessitated certain understandings about relationships with others: wariness, circumvention, avoidance, and fear. Not only was one aware that extralegal behavior was necessary and was the norm, but one was also especially aware of the fact that such behavior was extralegal. A common-sense world of rules of behavior arose for those in this situation, which allowed them to condemn certain forms of personal behavior while condoning private actions that were "wrong" under the legal code. They stole openly: some people stole only from state enterprises; some people took extra materials home from their jobs in order to trade them for goods and services similarly taken from other jobs by other people. Some protected their neighbors' right to engage in such criminal behavior against the government by turning a blind eye to such behavior. The choice, as to the amount of involvement with each particular act, was difficult since each person answered to his or her own sense of right and wrong in a system where right and wrong were not clearly defined for the population by a legal code adhered to by the majority and sufficiently enforced to suggest official concern about violations of the code.

Because there were so many variations to "beating the system," the population developed techniques that protected them from having too much overt knowledge of criminal activities, while at the same time allowing them to maintain relationships with people whose standards of involvement were different. Additionally, this criminal activity was so pervasive and so apparent to the authorities (who were also involved but who are charged with law enforcement) that the population developed great sensitivity to nuances and situations--a sort of ever-present antenna that homed in on possible threats, real or imagined, to their extralegal activities.

In this bureaucratic system, where the government was the major employer, the giver of law, and the taker of liberty, one had to become skillful in manipulating those bureaucratic officials who had the power to make life difficult, often without appeal. These skills, useful in the manipulation of such contacts, became part of the techniques of living, part of the social order understood by members of the new Russian immigration.

Therefore, in the USSR, crime is an underlying basic aspect of Soviet life: secrecy, corruption, theft, and cover-ups are constant factors in day-to-day activity. Because of this, members of Russian society were pulled in opposite directions on a daily basis. They were pulled between bureaucratic goals in a bureaucratic system ostensibly structured with guidelines and constraints, which despite their ideology, force the members of the society toward contravention of the stated principles of the state. In fact, a criminogenic ethic is created.

Years of socialization in the understandings, skills and behavior necessary for existence in the Soviet system, where the general informal system of understanding permitted behavior contrary to the "established" legal code without necessarily invoking the sanctions of one's compatriots, created a moral order within which one could "beat the system" without invoking moral or legal sanctions.

One can understand the behavior of this immigrant population in their home country because of the ongoing difficulty in obtaining necessary goods and services. There, one believed that "everyone was doing it" and lived so as to circumvent sanctions against people involved in extralegal behavior. This lifetime of learning not only concerned the acquisition of goods and services, but also the behaviors of friends and foes.

What we have studied is a population that has immigrated from a society in which a very large number of its ordinary citizens see what is officially defined as crime as an ordinary and not immoral response. We have thus viewed crime as normal within the Soviet system and have gone on to examine how the new immigrant reacts to life in a society where the official, public value system is not as deeply corrupted and permeated by acceptable crime. The question asked in this study is whether easier access to goods and services changes the attitudes created by a lifetime of criminal behavior for the acquisition of ordinary goods and services. That is, after a lifetime of training and socialization in one system, can the new immigrant learn to reinterpret the expectations and understandings permitted and approved in the new social order?

The answer to this question--whether easier access to goods and services changed the lifetime learnings of the "new" Russian population--is that such changes, if they do occur, will occur only very slowly. Examination of this population indicated that change of locale alone does not permit the relearning of understandings sufficiently to change behavior. The moral order, the common-sense world of rules, is not easily cast aside after a lifetime of habituation to it. Skills learned and utilized in order to "beat the system" are still operant after immigration. Changing one's address does not change one's interpretation of situations. The understandings with which new Russian immigrants conducted life in the USSR still continue to govern their conduct in the United States. The homeland techniques of guarded interpretation of nuances and situations are still used when these immigrants come into contact with individuals and officials.

The new Russian immigrant interprets situations against a background of expectancies garnered through living in another system. The interpretations are often far different from the interpretations an American would use, even if both the American and the new Russian are viewing the same situation. Actions spurred by these interpretations also differ, as can be seen, for example, when a Russian is asked to submit papers to a governmental agency for stamping. To the Russian, versed in the understandings of the USSR, the very release of these papers into the hands of another creates a situation of extreme tension. To an American, the release of such papers into the hands of a bureaucratic clerk may also create tension; but the Russian's tension is the result of fear that the papers will not be returned for arbitrary reasons. For the American the tension may result from impatience and annoyance with long lines and inefficient bureaucracy. Rarely would the American consider the threat that the papers would not be returned.

Similarly, a clerk in an American fingerprint office dealing with new Russian immigrants would not assume that the person whose papers were waiting in a basket for processing would send another immigrant for fingerprinting on the papers of the first. For the clerk this is an impersonal, nonthreatening matter, where guile and intrigue are unnecessary. For the Russian, guile and intrigue are part of the interpretations and understandings involved in dealing with the situation. Situations are understood against a background of expectations and previously learned techniques of interpretation.

People's responses to present situations are based on their previous experiences. They next decide what action is appropriate in order to achieve the desired results, then they act. Thus, putting one's papers in a basket for pickup, for an American, involves few major social judgments. There is also no need for the average American to manipulate the situation in order to produce some kind of results beyond those immediately expected. Manipulation is not needed. The views of a foreigner facing the same situation against the same background contingencies depends on the foreigner's previous learnings in the old country. This cultural template, this expectation of results from specific actions, is not directly translatable from one culture to another. In some circumstances the results of actions in one country are the same as in another; in other circumstances the results are different. Thus what is, for the new Russian, often an ordinary response to understandings and to situations, in this country may be viewed as far from the ordinary understanding and response of a native American.

For the new Russian immigrant, the moral order of the past is not easy to cast aside. Older techniques of interpretation of nuances and situations still operate.

I have examined the new Russian immigrants and their adaptations of their coping techniques to life in the United States, and conclude that it is not the behavior of the immigrants that differs after immigration, but rather the interpretation of that behavior by significant others differs. For example, in her homeland the Russian woman on the street would think nothing about commenting about the public behavior of another. Such comments are part of everyday life in the Soviet Union. "It is not cultured to take pictures of strangers on the street," she would say to someone pointing a camera. To do so here on the street, to a stranger, would not evoke tolerant behavior or even understanding of how someone is provoked to so act. Rather, such behavior here might be viewed as "crazy" or "picking a fight." It is possible that upon immigration the new immigrant remains as involved in the same kind of actions as previously, but the responses of the society, the government, and the bureaucracy in the United States are different. Some actions that were illegal there are legal here. Behavior accepted there is not accepted here. Understandings operant there are out of kilter here. Circumvention of certain governmental agencies, necessary there, proves to be not only unnecessary here but sometimes foolish. Criminal activities conducted there are accepted business practices here. Other criminal activities conducted there are so "foreign" to our law-enforcement officials that initial confusion results; for example, the man whose car was confiscated by a government agency, who then reported it stolen to another government agency. This type of understanding would not be part of an American's understanding, criminal or not. Actions acceptable there, but illegal here, arouse suspicion in Americans. Behavior seems to change less because of immigration than because of the interpretation of that behavior against the social understandings of the new society.

Theories of immigrant crime, based on an earlier immigration, have suggested that it is our American system that creates, out of an immigrant, a person who has to engage in illegal behavior in order to succeed. Basically, there are two distinct theories applicable to the immigrant. Merton, and subsequently Bell, see factors in the very nature of American society that channel some individuals to achieve social goals through inappropriate, not socially acceptable, means. For Bell in particular, immigrants, new to an established social order, without the skills or abilities to provide for themselves and their families, resort to extralegal means for achieving success in the new system. Only in this way are they able to rise on the social ladder of measured American success, that is, to obtain money, prestige, and material goods. Thus, in order to get a foothold on the ladder of American success the newcomer to this land becomes a marginal enterpreneur, who provides for a hungry population items that are not available through legitimate channels. This follows Merton's theory of social structure and anomie. For him, it is clear that if one is unable to conform to the nature of social structure of a particular society, if one is unable to compete and derive satisfaction from such competition within the established social order, then one devises other ways to be competitive; crime is just one such way to succeed. This approach to crime and the immigrant rests on the Anglo-Saxon vision of success, i.e., hard work, learning, cleanliness. The immigrant's hard work and personal habits are much reflected in these views of crime causation.

The other group of theorists, including Sutherland, Shaw, and McKay, saw urbanization and industrialization plus the immigration of a large population from Eastern Europe as weakening our forms of social control--which, like our population, had been predominately Anglo-Saxon. To them, the slums of these immi-grants were themselves repositories of cultural traditions that moved the new populations into extralegal behavior patterns. These theorists suggest that immigrants, arriving humble, poor, and unable to enter into middle-class areas of their new nation, settle into crowded neighborhoods where life is difficult. These ghettos--where mothers and fathers allow their children to get lost on the streets, where life is disorganized, and where apartments in deplorable condition house armies of the unwashed and unskilled--create new values. These values, as Sutherland theorizes, are favorable to the commission of crime. Children growing up in such conditions acquire a preponderance of criminal values. Social order is weak in areas of social diversity and, since waves of immigrations succeeded waves of immigrations into the same city neighborhoods, an ethic was created favoring criminal enterprises, often because these were the only forms of enterprise available to such populations.

Both sets of theorists seem to see factors and situations in this country as providing causation for immigrant crime. Inferentially, both view immigrant crime as originating here in the new land. Specifically, there is no accounting for the culture of the first group of immigrants who reached these shores. Could they have adapted behavior in order to function in the boundaries of their new society so quickly? Both groups of theorists suggest that marginality and/or the culture of the slum provide fertile ground for the creation of new behavior patterns. It would appear that only the marginal, the poor, and those unskilled in the proficiencies necessary for entrance into the American economy have been studied. The early immigrants came to an industrial nation and functioned against an unfamiliar urban backdrop, which presented totally unfamiliar schemata to the unskilled and agrarian immigrants about whom most of the literature is concerned.

This is not so with the population studied. The new Russian immigrant in Brighton Beach lives in conditions physically similar to those left behind--Odessa is on the sea and is urban. Although apartment living is less crowded in Brighton and the stores have a larger selection of available merchandise, there is an ambience remarkably similar to what the immigrants are used to. This population is not as marginal as the earlier immigrants: not housed in economic ghettos and able, in many instances, to enter the job market in occupations which, if not exactly identical, are similar to those followed in the USSR. More important, the new Russian immigrants learned their "criminal" behavior prior to their entry into this country. Their understandings about how one deals with the law, with bureaucracy, and with those engaged in illegality, predated their immigration. Rather than learning criminal patterns in order to ascend through the strata of American society, these immigrants arrived with cultural traditions they had learned

through old-world associations with others, which favored violation
of legal codes. Daniel Bell describes crime as "in many ways . . . a
Coney Island mirror, caricaturing the morals and manners of a
society."[1] It is this caricature of morals and manners of the
homeland which has immigrated to Brighton Beach. For although
Bell was referring to the "brawling nature of American
development" and the "jungle quality of the American business
community,"[2] the new immigrants learned their crime in a society
across the ocean. Where Bell described his immigrant as different
from the older, Protestant American whose "intense acquisitiveness
. . . was rationalized by a compulsive moral fervor,"[3] the new
Russian immigrant comes with a tradition of acquisitiveness
necessitated by life in a society where the lack of goods and
services created an underground economy, which provided those
necessities for a price and where social morality accepted this
behavior. Bell attributes much of this criminality to a desire for
the forbidden fruits of conventional morality. He maintains that
there is more to this: for it is through the avenues of criminality
that one can move into what he sees as a unique aspect of the
openness of American society--a business of one's own and a way to
move up the social ladder through a marginal business and through
relationship of this marginal business to the political machine of
the day.

But the new Russian immigrants developed traits that continue
to operate after immigration, traits involving circumvention and
criminality. Their proneness to crime developed not as a result of
the American success ethic or America's unique openness--which
for Bell characterized American society--but rather as a result of
quite the opposite. They, too, hunted for forbidden fruits, but not
of conventional American Protestant morality. Rather, their
conventional morality allowed them to engage in pursuits that
provided them with those forbidden fruits. Whereas Bell asserted
that crime is an American way of life, revitalized with each new
group of immigrants--who, upon reaching these shores, begin an
illegal ascent into the ranks of a criminal culture--here we have an
example of a group of immigrants who arrived with criminal
patterns already in place--to such an extent that they already
engaged in crime. Where Bell saw crime in the United States as the
result of certain characteristics in the American economy, in
American ethnic groups, and in American policy, we have examined
it as based on certain characteristics in the Soviet economy and
Soviet policy. What we see is that the morals and manners of the
new Russian immigrant continue to operate against the new
background of life in the United States.

The new Russian immigrant arrived on these shores already
steeped in a criminal system, already one rung up on the ladder of
social mobility, and with certain skills already in place. It is the
conclusion of this study that these immigrants did not change their

behavior to ascend the American social ladder. Rather, they continued patterns of behavior that were ingrained after a lifetime in a social system where extralegal values were stressed for reasons beyond those considered part of the American ethic. Money and success, often viewed as the goal of the American system for which means of achievement have not always been provided, underlie much of the theory of causation of criminality. But here we have a population which was, and in many cases continues to be, involved in criminality for reasons beyond those cited by previous theorists.

Of particular interest is how, upon immigration, these unique immigrants adapt their lifetime learnings to a society that is, in many respects, similar to the one they left. These immigrants are primarily of urban background. They have lived in a society where relatively high technology is an economic fact; subsequently they have moved to another industrial technological society. Often they bring skills that are much in demand in the marketplace. They understand the Russian version of bureaucracy because they have existed in a 24-hour-a-day bureaucracy in Russia, opposed to the part-time bureaucracy here. They understand how to manipulate and circumvent Soviet-style bureaucracies because they have had a lifetime of training in such behavior. They continue their ways here in as many places and situations as they can. Here, the surrounding society employs them in legitimate enterprises; there, identical behavior would mean participating in illegality. Here, too, it is the surrounding bureaucracy that provides or refuses to provide them entitlements, which they see as governmental dole, of which they want or do not want a part.

How then do these immigrants, who grew up in a society favoring extralegal values, adapt to life in a society where these values are less needed? To repeat, immigrants understand the society they have entered only with the cultural learnings of the society they have left; their understandings are brought with them. An American law-enforcement agent who calls for an appointment is thus understood not to be as tough as one who breaks down the door. Government is never one's friend. But when government agencies do not prosecute violent crime, they are criticized for excessive leniency. Due process for criminals is understood to be weakness on the part of governmental agencies. Bureaucratic entitlements are understood as a given right, to be taken wherever possible. Trust is hard to gain, and one has to be constantly vigilant when dealing with all but the most familiar. One has to be aware of the activities around one at all times, and often one is surrounded by people who are not friendly. Paper is important, and manipulation of it is a part of existence. These are operant understandings that migrate with the immigrant.

It is my contention that it is not the immigrants who change their understandings, behavior, and actions as a result of immigration, but rather they bring with them their own moral code, developed in a far-away land, with which to analyze situations here. In some instances, their codes mesh with those of the surrounding society, and in some instances, they do not. Those who were engaged in behavior which, although criminal, was of utmost necessity for day-to-day survival, those who in this study are called the survivors, continue to use just as much extralegal behavior as needed for survival in their new land. Since much of their behavior there was not such as to be considered criminal here, these people may move out of their criminality into legitimate endeavors. They still maintain those skills and understandings with which they came armed, but their need for them may lessen in time. If they succeed in their new "legality," they may become socialized to American patterns of legality and illegality (white-collar crime). It is likely that such a transformation of consciousness may take more than one generation.

On the other hand, those whose existence in the USSR was totally extralegal, whose interest in criminality was beyond that needed to support their family or their place at work, will also continue their illegal behavior upon immigration. These, referred to in this study as the connivers, were engaged in trades and business that are continued after immigration in criminal activities of the same sort as they were engaged in in Russia. Burglary, arson, counterfeiting, and fencing of goods continue to occupy their time, and their contacts continue to be with those who are and were engaged in similar pursuits. Additionally, with the ease of travel, the open state of borders, and the "naivete" of government agents, connivers are able not only to continue but to excel in their criminal career. They manipulate papers, move currency (both real and counterfeit), deal in credit and credit cards, and generally have at their disposal a wide avenue of illegal pursuits, unhampered as yet by powerful governmental interference. It is the conclusion of this study that the behavior of the new Russian immigrants and their criminality (with exceptions noted) does not change upon immigration but rather that it is the public interpretation of this behavior, its characterization as legal or illegal, that determines whether the new Russian immigrant is a criminal.

Further research is required, for this is indeed a large area for study. It is suggested that the very ease of travel, the ability to manipulate international markets and currency, diamonds, and drugs suggests that the day of studying criminality in only one jurisdiction is over. Criminals versed in world travel and skilled in movement, like the sophisticated new Russian criminal, are already making their presence known internationally. The extent and degree of organization of such criminal activities cannot as yet be fully assessed. More time, more development, and much more research will be necessary to assess this latter area. Last, it is of interest to discover how some people are able to maintain their own personal value system and their own state of morality while living in a society where every current moves one further toward some kind of criminal behavior. This resistance disproves all the conventional theory.

NOTES

1 Bell, p. 132.

2 Ibid.

3 Ibid.

Index